SUCCESSFUL INDOOR GARDENING

EXOTIC
CACTI

Peter Chapman and Margaret Martin

HPBooks
a division of
PRICE STERN SLOAN
Los Angeles

A Salamander Book

©1989 by Salamander Books Ltd.,
52 Bedford Row, London WC1R 4LR,
United Kingdom.

Published by HPBooks, a division of Price Stern Sloan, Inc.
360 North La Cienega Boulevard, Los Angeles, California 90048.
Printed in Belgium.

9 8 7 6 5 4 3 2 1

Library of Congress Cataloging-in-Publication Data

Chapman, Peter R. (Peter Richard)
    Exotic cacti / by Peter Chapman and Margaret Martin.
        p.   cm — (Successful indoor gardening)
    Includes index.
    ISBN 0-89586-832-6 : $9.95 ($12.95 Can.)
    1. Cactus.   I. Martin, Margaret J.   II. Title.   III. Series.
SB438.C38   1989   89-2094
635.9'3347—dc19   CIP

Credits

Introduction written by: David Squire
Editor: Geoffrey Rogers
Assistant editor: Lisa Dyer
Designer: Paul Johnson
Photographs: Picture credits appear on page 96
Line artwork: Maureen Holt
Filmset by: The Old Mill, London
Color separation by: Kentscan Ltd.
Printed by: Proost International Book Production, Turnhout, Belgium

Contents

Introduction	6
Easy to Grow	14
Moderately Easy to Grow	52
Difficult to Grow	86
Index	95

Introduction

Cacti are amongst the most popular of all indoor plants, not least because they can withstand relatively long periods of neglect which makes them ideal for busy or forgetful growers. This highly informative book contains over 75 of the more exotic varieties of cactus, many of which are illustrated in full colour with a stunning photograph of the plant in bloom. The cacti are grouped according to the ease with which they can be grown and detailed growing instructions include such essential information as the water, light and temperature requirements of each species.

The Cactus family
Cacti belong exlusively to the Cactaceae family. They are characterized by having areoles (resembling small pincushions) from which spines, short hooks or long and woolly hairs grow. Flowers and stems also develop from the areoles. Another characteristic of the family is that, with the exception of pereskias and young opuntias, none of the members bears leaves.

   With one exception — the pereskias — all cacti belong to a larger group of plants called succulents. These plants have the ability to store water in their fleshy leaves and stems, and are usually native to arid regions of the world. They include a wide range of different plant families, of which the Cactaceae is but one.

   Cacti, often referred to as stem succulents, are divided into two groups: desert types, whose natural environment is the warm, semi-desert regions of the American continent; and forest types which come from the forest regions of tropical America. An exception is *Rhipsalis baccifera* which is native to Africa and Sri Lanka as well as America. Forest types can be easily distinguished from desert

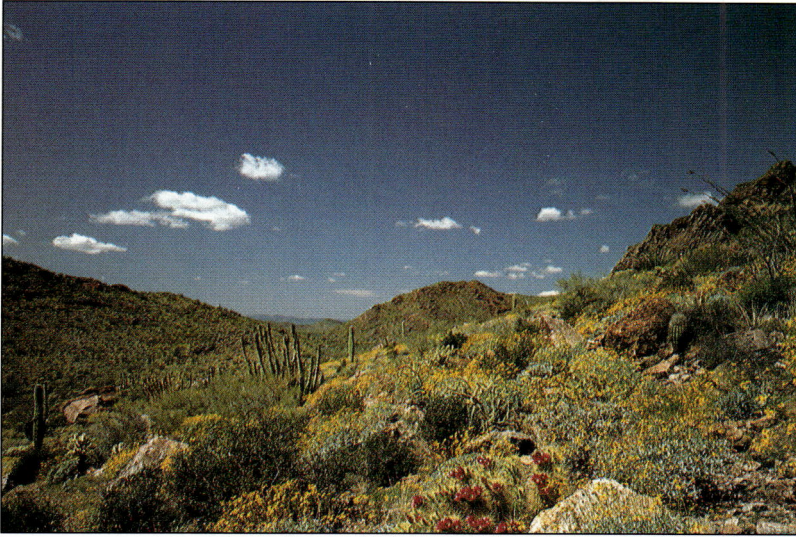

Below left: Spines, hooks or long and woolly hairs characterize cacti. Here, a ferocactus reveals its protective, stout spines.

Above: These desert cacti, in their natural habitat, display a wealth of colour, as well as an amazing range of shapes and sizes.

types by their trailing habit and, with many species such as the Christmas cactus, by their flattened and segmented stems.

Forest cacti live as epiphytes, attached to trees where they gain support but do not take nourishment from their host. They are not so numerous as desert types but include many well known species such as the Christmas cactus (*Schlumbergera 'Buckleyi'*), the orchid cactus (*Epiphyllum* sp.) and the well-known rat's tail cactus (*Aporocactus flagelliformis*). Confusingly, although the rat's tail cactus is a forest type, it is best treated as a desert type. Desert cacti include such well known species as the silver torch (*Cleistocactus strausii*), the golden barrel cactus (*Echinocactus grusonii*) and the peanut cactus (*Chamaecereus silvestrii*).

Buying cacti

When you first buy them, cacti are usually much smaller than other plants, but just as much care is needed in their selection as with other plant types. Cacti tend to be specialists' plants and, as well as being sold through garden centres, they can be bought from specialist nurseries which offer an even wider range of species. To ensure success with cacti, follow these simple guidelines.

▫ Buy plants from reputable sources.
▫ Don't buy plants which are unlabelled. Reputable nurseries always label their plants clearly.
▫ Don't buy cacti which are displayed outside shops in winter — although most desert cacti prefer low winter temperatures, cold winds and unpredictable low temperatures soon kill them. Cold shocks to forest cacti may cause flower buds to fall off or not develop properly.
▫ Don't buy plants infested with pests or diseases. Not only will the plants be marred, they will infect others.
▫ Don't buy plants with algae or slime on the compost or pot. As well as being unsightly, this indicates that the plant has been in the pot for a long time and has probably been watered excessively.

Above: Forest cacti are not as abundant as desert types, but are equally attractive. They trail from branches, creating spectacular displays of flowers and stems.

Right: Greenhouses provide a cool, dry and airy environment for cacti during winter. Warm and humid conditions indoors at this time of the year soon damage the plants.

Getting cacti home

Because cacti tend to be smaller than other houseplants, it is generally much easier to get them home safely: just follow these three recommendations.

☐ Make buying cacti the last job on your shopping list. There is then less chance of them becoming damaged — or injuring you through their spines!

☐ Avoid putting plants in extremely cold car boots (trunks) in winter, or in hot boots in summer. Instead, stand them in shallow boxes placed inside the car, but safe from the ravages of young children or dogs.

☐ Get your cacti home as quickly as possible, especially in winter.

Acclimatizing new plants

Once you have got your new plant home you should quickly establish it indoors by immediately placing it in its permanent position, in good light. Be careful positioning the Christmas cactus — you should avoid knocking it as this will cause the flower buds to drop off. If you have bought a forest cactus in flower be sure to keep the compost moist.

Getting the Best from Cacti

The pleasure you get from a cactus — and the time it remains attractive — depends on the way you care for it. Cacti are relatively tolerant plants but they should not be totally neglected, particularly if they are to be induced to flower.

Forest cacti are grown mainly for their flowers, but they are frequently shy to bloom, especially if they are denied a cool resting period. If treated properly, most desert cacti can be induced to flower by the time they are a few years old. Some, however, will not develop flowers until they are quite large, while others refuse to bloom under ordinary conditions indoors.

Here are a few ways to help you get the best from your cacti. Be sure you know which type you are caring for as desert cacti and forest cacti require different treatments.

Caring for Desert Cacti

Watering In Spring, increase the amount of water given to each plant. Soak the compost thoroughly when it becomes dry, especially during warm summer months, but take care not to keep it continually saturated. In late summer, reduce the frequency of watering and by mid-autumn apply only enough water to prevent the plant shrivelling. Continue in this way through winter until the following spring, when the temperature naturally rises, there is better natural sunlight and plants start to grow again. Desert cacti should never be mist-sprayed. Moisture which rests on a plant, especially in winter, could cause the onset of diseases and decay.

Extremely cold water can chill cacti, especially in winter — either use tepid water or allow the water to reach room temperature by allowing it to stand overnight.

Feeding Specific information is given in the growing instructions for each plant, but generally cacti benefit from a weak liquid feed — of the high-potassium type used for tomatoes — every two weeks from the time when the flower buds appear.

Temperature Almost all desert cacti can be overwintered at a temperature of 5°C (41°F) if the compost is kept relatively dry. Indeed, cacti which are grown for their display of flowers need a cold period to encourage them to bloom during the following year. The windowsill of a relatively cool or unheated room offers a good winter position, but avoid this position if the window is single-glazed and the weather outside is particularly cold. Other cacti, such as the hairy types, require warmer winter conditions.

In summer, the temperature will naturally rise, but avoid positions which are exceptionally hot. The uppermost temperatures individual cacti like are given for each species.

Compost Special mixtures of compost for cacti are widely available from garden centres. Rapid drainage is one of the ideals of cacti compost, but the compost should not be so full of sand that water runs straight through and out again.

Repotting When young, cacti should be repotted annually, but thereafter only when the compost becomes packed with roots. Repotting is best done in spring.

Light and air Choose a sunny position, such as a bright windowsill, especially in winter. Indoors, cacti do not need to be shaded, but if grown in a very bright greenhouse or conservatory, light shading may be needed during hot summer days. Plenty of fresh air is essential, especially in summer. Indeed, some cacti prefer outside conditions in summer to a hot stuffiness indoors.

Caring for Forest Cacti

Watering Because some forest cacti flower in winter, others in spring and a few in summer, their resting periods are different. This influences the time of year when water is needed. Therefore, these plants have to be treated individually and specific requirements are given in the instruction for each species. If your tap water is hard, use either rain water or water which has been boiled and allowed to cool. Unlike desert cacti, you should mist spray the stems regularly, especially in summer, but avoid water splashing on the flowers.

Temperature When forest cacti are growing, temperatures rising to 21°C (70°F) are suitable, especially if the atmosphere is humid. During the plant's resting period, however, keep the temperature to around 10-13°C (50-55°F).

Compost The compost should not be so sandy and free-draining as the mixture used for desert cacti. The best type of compost for individual species is suggested in the growing instructions for each plant.

Repotting Repot forest cacti annually, shortly after the flowering period has finished. However, epiphyllums flower best when their roots are constricted, so do not repot them too frequently.

Light and air Because forest cacti grow amid trees and are slightly shaded by them, they must not be positioned in strong sunlight. Choose a bright position, shaded from direct sunlight but with plenty of fresh air. Epiphyllums benefit from a position on an east-facing windowsill. Bear in mind when positioning forest cacti that they need to be placed somewhere where their trailing stems will not become damaged by passers-by.

Displaying Cacti

Cacti have a unique charm and, if well cared for, individual plants will grow quite large and remain with you for many years. Some have even been known to outlive their owners! It is therefore important to display them to their best advantage so that they form an attractive feature in a room.

Group displays Frequently, desert cacti are removed from their pots and planted in ornamental shallow containers. Some containers are only 25cm (10in) long with room for five or six small plants; others are up to 60cm (2ft) long and are planted to form a miniature landscape. You should take care when moving large or long containers as the combined weight of compost and plant may cause them to snap.

In greenhouses and conservatories, desert cacti are frequently planted to cover a large area. This is an excellent way to grow them as it helps to prevent individual plants being excessively watered. However, after a few years, one or two of the plants usually become dominant and have to be pruned or removed. But this is a small price to pay for the pleasure of having a landscape full of cacti.

Indoor hanging baskets Desert cacti are best grown in pots and displayed on a level surface. Forests types, however, naturally trail or cascade from trees and are therefore ideal for growing in indoor hanging baskets. The rat's tail cactus creates a spectacular display with its round, rat's tail like stems covered with vivid cerise flowers. The Christmas cactus also looks particularly good cascading out of indoor hanging baskets or pots positioned at the edges of high shelves.

Below: While young, small cacti can be attractively planted in ornate containers, and positioned on windowsills or tables near windows. Eventually, some of them outgrow and dominate the container; at this stage, repot them individually into small pots.

Displays in alcoves Small recesses with plain, preferably white or light-coloured backgrounds create superb places in which to display cascading forest cacti. Indoor hanging baskets also create an eye-catching feature in an alcove. Remember that the cactus may need to be removed from its flowering position when the flowers fade and placed in a cool spot where it can commence its resting period.

Cache pots Unlike most other indoor plants, few cacti are ever placed in cache pots. Also, if the growing pots are put inside cache pots, it is all too easy to give the plants too much water. In winter, water-saturated compost can prove fatal.

Windowsill displays Most cacti are grown and displayed on windowsills. Rather than putting the pots directly on the sill, they should be placed in a long, shallow plastic tray. Kitchen windowsills, where light is generally good, make particularly good homes for cacti.

Above: Woolly aphids sometimes infest cacti. They cluster around the base of spines and resemble blobs of white, waxy wool.

Below: Dactylopius coccus is the species of cactus-eating scale insect from which the dye cochineal is derived.

Good Health Guide

Cacti are relatively trouble-free, but there are some pests, diseases and physiological disorders which can seriously affect them. Here are the ones which you will mainly encounter.

Cacti infesting pests

☐ **Mealy bugs** are, perhaps, the major pest which infests cacti. They are slow-moving — eventually static — pests which resemble small, woolly woodlice. They cluster in the softest part of a cactus, making it extremely unsightly. Minor infestations can be cleared by using a small brush dipped in methylated spirits. Alternatively, you can water the compost with an insecticide.

☐ **Root mealy bugs** These are pernicious pests, related to ordinary mealy bugs and resembling small woodlice. They chew the roots of plants in pots and upset normal root functions; the roots are damaged and plants wilt and eventually die. To eradicate these pests, drench the compost with a systemic insecticide.

☐ **Red spider mites** occasionally infest cacti, especially if the weather is exceptionally hot and the air dry. They may even create webbing over the plants. Use a systemic insecticide to control them.

☐ **Root knot eelworm** is a pest of greenhouse and conservatory plants, occasionally attacking cacti. The eelworms cause galls on the roots, which disturbs the plant's intake of water. Destroy infected plants and discard the compost where it cannot re-infect other plants.

☐ **Woolly aphids** These are similar in appearance to their relatives the aphid (or greenfly), except they are covered with a protective white, waxy wool. They occasionally infest cacti where they attack soft joints and the base of spines. Use a small brush dipped in methylated spirits to wipe away minor infestations and a systemic insecticide to remove larger colonies. True aphids rarely attack cacti.

☐ **Scale insects** These pests infest neglected cacti, often encrusting them in scales. A tropical and sub-tropical American species produces the red dye cochineal. Wipe away slight infestations and use a systemic insecticide on severe attacks.

Cacti diseases

☐ **Viruses** invade some cacti, especially epiphyllums, causing yellow or, occasionally, purple spots. This virus also affects the flowers, which may develop striped and broken colours. Viruses are notoriously difficult to eradicate — if not impossible. Therefore, it is wise to ensure that all plants you buy are free from viruses. Buy cacti only from reputable sources and, if they become badly infected, remove and burn them.

☐ **Corky scab** reveals itself as rusty or corky spots on stems — the result of damaged tissue — and affected areas soon shrivel and sink. There is no cure and infected plants should be destroyed. This disease especially affects opuntias and epiphyllums.

Physiological disorders These occur because a plant has not been given the correct treatment. One example is the plant collapsing and eventually rotting. This can occur if it has been excessively watered, especially in winter when there is no active growing and the temperature is low. The tops of plants become discoloured and eventually collapse. Mammillarias are particularly susceptible to this.

Easy to Grow

The range of cacti is very wide and there are many which are easy to grow, even for the most inexperienced growers of houseplants. Indeed, if you are considering creating your first-ever collection of plants, you cannot go wrong with the cacti featured in this section. And even if you have only a kitchen windowsill, it will still be possible to grow many different species.

Within these easy-to-grow plants there are both desert and forest types. Forest types include the rat's tail cactus (*Aporocactus flagelliformis*) and the Christmas cactus (*Schlumbergera 'Buckleyi'*), both of which bear attractive flowers. The desert cacti include flowering types as well as those grown for their column-like stance or wealth of long white hairs or spines.

period. Repot annually. Never allow the plant to become completely dry, even in winter. In summer, water generously.

When the plant becomes too large, one of the tails may be cut off, dried for two days and potted up. Early summer is the best time for rooting cuttings. Mealy bug can be a serious pest. It is easy to overlook them on a large plant. Treat the plant with a systemic insecticide.

Take care
Never let this plant dry out.

- Diffuse sunlight
- Temp: 5-30°C (41-86°F)
- Keep moist all year

Aporocactus flagelliformis
RAT'S-TAIL CACTUS

A beautiful plant for a hanging basket, this cactus will grow happily in a window. The long slender stems may reach a length of 2m (6.5ft); they are closely ribbed and densely covered with small brown spines. In early spring, the stems are covered with vivid cerise flowers; these are tubular, 5cm (2in) long, and last for several days.

A loam- or peat-based mixture is suitable for this plant. Feed with a liquid tomato fertilizer once every two weeks during the growing

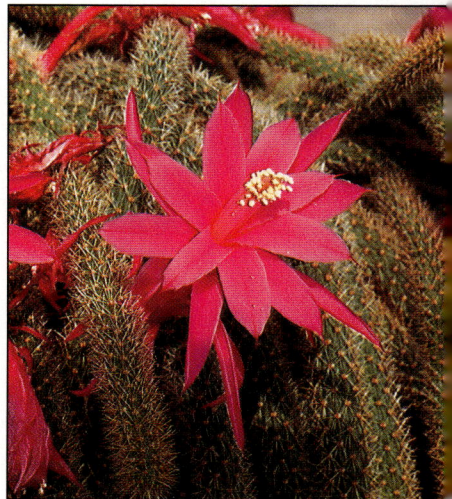

in short spines. In early summer, large numbers of brilliant red flowers are carried along the stems.

A good loam- or peat-based mixture is needed. Repot annually. During the summer growing period, water generously and use a liquid tomato fertilizer every two weeks.

Aporocactus mallisonii (now known as x *Heliaporus smithii*) is a hybrid and can only be propagated vegetatively. When the plant has outgrown its accommodation, cut off one of the stems. Dry for two days and pot up. Propagation is most successful in early summer. Mealy bug is the chief pest that attacks this cactus. Inspect the stems regularly. Spray with a proprietary insecticide if an infestation is found.

Take care
Never let this plant dry out.

Aporocactus mallisonii

An excellent plant for a hanging basket, this cactus will thrive in a warm living-room but does need plenty of light. The stout stems reach a length of about 1m (39in); they are deeply ribbed and covered

☐ Diffuse sunlight
☐ Temp: 5-30°C (41-86°F)
☐ Keep damp all year

Left: The popular rat's tail cactus, Aporocactus flagelliformis, has long, hanging stems and colourful flowers. It is a 'must' for an indoor hanging basket.

Above: Aporocactus mallisonii is an ideal plant for growing in an indoor hanging basket. It develops trailing stems and large red flowers in early summer.

Cereus peruvianus
APPLE CACTUS
PERUVIAN APPLE
PERUVIAN APPLE CACTUS
TORCH CACTUS

This columnar plant forms a handsome addition to any cactus collection. It is a vigorous plant and in a matter of a few years will form a blue-green column about 2m (6.5ft) high. The stem is ribbed, and the ribs carry stout spines. It is possible to flower this cereus in cultivation; the large white flowers open at night. In the wild, this plant will reach a height of 9m (30ft). When it reaches the roof of the greenhouse, cut the cereus about 1m (39in) from the top, dry for three days, and then pot up the top. The base will send out branches, which can be used for propagation.

Grow in a loam-based mixture and repot annually. Water generously during summer, and feed about once a month with a liquid fertilizer with a high potassium content (tomato fertilizer). Keep dry in winter. *C. peruvianus* is tough and vigorous, and unlikely to be bothered by pests.

Take care
Do not allow this plant to become potbound.

- □ Full sun
- □ Temp: 5-30°C (41-86°F)
- □ Water generously in summer

Above: The peanut cactus, Chamaecereus silvestrii, is a very popular species. During spring and summer, finger-like stems bear brilliantly coloured flowers.

Chamaecereus silvestrii
PEANUT CACTUS

Sometimes listed as *Lobivia silvestrii* (another victim of botanical name changes), it seems more appropriate here to use the name of so many years standing. The spreading stems are somewhat finger-like in shape and size, bright green in colour and covered with short spines. Offsets, somewhat resembling green peanuts, appear along the length of the stems, hence the popular name. They

detach themselves at the slightest touch, and can be potted up at once — surely the easiest cactus to propagate! But the great joy of this plant is the brilliant scarlet flowers, 4cm (1.6in) across; produced in profusion, they almost cover the stems during spring and summer.

This is not a fussy plant, so grow it in any good potting mixture. Water freely in spring and summer. One of the hardiest cacti, it will survive in a cold frame if quite dry.

Take care
Keep cold in winter to encourage good flowering.

- Full sun
- Temp: 0-30°C (32-86°F)
- Keep dry in winter

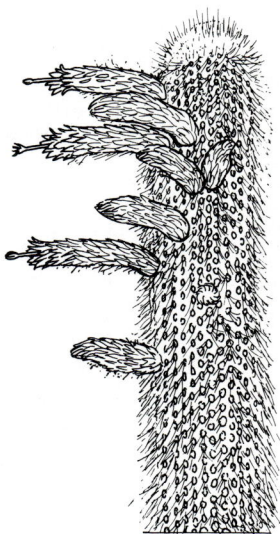

Cleistocactus strausii
SILVER TORCH

Cleistocactus strausii is a slender column that will reach a height of 2m (6.5ft); the stem branches from the base. The plant is densely covered in short white spines, which give the plant a silvery gleam in the sunlight. Mature specimens flower freely in cultivation. The carmine flowers are carried on the sides of the columns and have a very characteristic shape; they consist of a long narrow tube with an opening only large enough for the stamens to protrude.

   This is a vigorous cactus and to keep healthy it needs a good loam-based mixture and an annual repotting. Water generously during summer, give an occasional high-potassium liquid feed, and keep it dry in winter. To encourage flowering, put it in the sunniest position available. Some of the stems may be removed and used as cuttings if the plant is becoming too crowded.

Take care
Do not let this cactus become potbound.

□ Full sun
□ Temp: 5-30°C (41-86°F)
□ Water generously in summer

Echinocactus grusonii

BARREL CACTUS
GOLDEN BALL
GOLDEN BALL CACTUS
GOLDEN BARREL

Young specimens of *E. grusonii* have very pronounced tubercles and look like golden mammillaria. After a few years, the tubercles re-arrange themselves into ribs, usually about 28 per plant. *E. grusonii* is very long-lived and eventually reaches a diameter

Left: Cleistocactus strausii forms beautiful silvery columns which often grow over 1m (39in) high, but it is unlikely to out-grow its welcome in the average collection. Branches usually form at the base. Small flowers are produced on older plants, but do not open fully.

of 1m (39in). But in cultivation a plant of 15cm (6in) is a good-sized specimen and will be about 10 years old. The awl-shaped spines are pale golden-yellow and there is golden wool at the top of the plant. The small yellow flowers are produced on very large plants but only if exposed to very strong sunlight. In cooler climates, this plant is grown purely for the beauty of its colouring.

It needs an open soil, a loam- or peat-based mixture plus one third sharp sand or perlite. Water generously during summer, but allow it to dry out between waterings. Keep dry in winter. The chief pests are mealy bug and root mealy bug.

Take care
Avoid a cold, damp atmosphere.

□ Full sun
□ Temp: 7-30°C (45-86°F)
□ Keep dry in winter

Below: Only large specimens of the barrel cactus, Echinocactus grusonii, will flower. Winter cold can cause brown markings, so keep this cactus warm.

Echinocereus pentalophus

The small upright stem of this cactus soon branches and the ultimate result is a mass of sprawling shoots up to about 12cm (4.7in) long and 2cm (0.8in) thick. The spines are quite short and soft. On the whole perhaps it is not a particularly striking plant, but the magnificent blooms more than compensate for any lack of beauty in the cactus itself. Quite small specimens (one stem) will produce reddish-purple flowers up to 8cm (3.2in) across.

The stems, being rather soft and fleshy, are prone to rot with any excess water, so it is particularly important to use a well-drained potting mixture with no risk of waterlogging. Make this by adding one part of sharp sand or perlite to two parts of a standard potting mxiture, which can be either peat- or loam-based. Propagate it by removing a suitable branch in summer, letting it dry for a few days, and potting up.

Take care
Water freely in summer.

□ Full sun
□ Temp: 5-30°C (41-86°F)
□ Keep dry in winter

Right: Echinocereus salm-dyckianus creates a mass of soft, branching stems, some sprawling. During mid-summer it bears beautiful, funnel-shaped flowers.

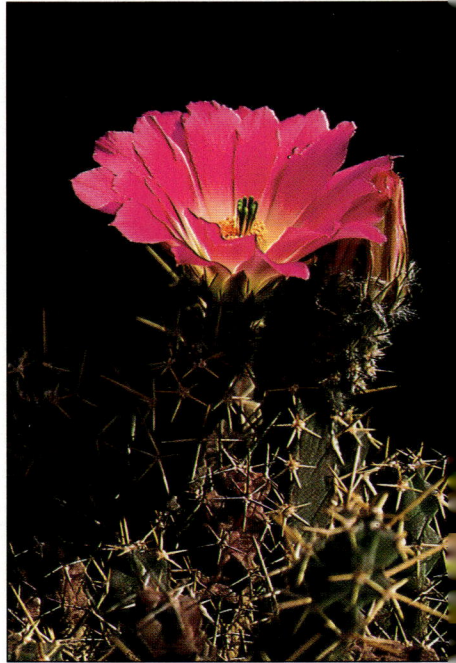

Above: Echinocereus pentalophus eventually forms a mass of sprawling stems. The eye-catching reddish-purple flowers are produced abundantly.

Echinocereus
salm-dyckianus

There are two types of echinocereus: those with fairly soft, mostly sprawling stems; and the pectinate (or comb-like) ones, with stiffer, elegantly spined, upright stems. This cactus belongs to the former group. Although small specimens consist of a single, upright stem, this soon branches at the base, eventually forming a clump of ribbed stems about 20cm (8in) long and 5cm (2in) thick, with short yellowish spines. It is probably the most attractive among the echinocerei, an attractiveness emphasized by the appearance of the funnel-shaped, orange flowers. These are about 7cm (2.8in) wide and can be up to 10cm (4in) long.

Grow in a mixture of one part sharp sand or perlite to two parts of any good standard material, to give the good drainage essential to this cactus. A gravel top dressing will protect the base. Feed every two weeks during the flowering season, to keep the flowers going.

Take care
Ensure a cold winter rest.

□ Full sun
□ Temp: 5-30°C (41-86°F)
□ Keep dry in winter

Above: Echinocereus websterianus has a bright green body with 20 ribs. Flowers — often wider than the plant — appear in summer, with green and yellow centres surrounded by eye-catching petals.

Echinocereus websterianus

Another delightful echinocereus from the pectinate (comb-like) group. This cactus has a bright green stem divided into about 20 narrow ribs; along the length of each are groups of short, stiff, spreading white spines. In its native southern USA it can become quite large, but a good pot specimen would be about 15cm (6in) high and 5cm (2in) thick; branches are not usually formed. Blooms can be as wide as the plant itself, but usually on smaller specimens only one appears at a time, opening from a large bristly bud. The green and yellow centre of the flower contrasts splendidly with the brightly coloured petals.

Make up a well-drained potting mixture by adding one third of extra sharp sand or perlite to any good standard mix. With this you can water freely in spring and summer. Give this echinocereus a cold winter rest to ensure next year's flowers. If it is part of a living room collection, try to overwinter it in an unheated room.

Take care
Check for root loss in winter.

☐ Full sun
☐ Temp: 5-30°C (41-86°F)
☐ Keep dry in winter

Echinofossulocactus lamellosus
BRAIN CACTUS

This group of cacti was formerly called *Stenocactus* and it is rather unfortunate that specialists have substituted the much longer name, if only because of the difficulty of writing it on a label! This is one of the prettiest, with a

Below: Echinofossulocactus lamellosus has a pretty, blue-green body and pink flowers which bloom during spring.

blue-green globular stem becoming rather cylindrical with age, and a diameter of up to 10cm (4in). The many thin ribs are wavy, which is characteristic of echinofossulocacti. White flattened spines are 1-3cm (0.4-1.2in) long, some curved upwards. This very attractive cactus will often produce its flowers when quite small; they are pink in colour, red inside, and tubular in shape, about 4cm (1.6in) long.

Coming as it does from sun-baked mountain regions, this plant can take all the sun you can give it in order to produce good spines and flowers. For this reason it is not so good as a houseplant. Water it freely in spring and summer, provided you grow it in a porous potting mixture of one part sharp sand or perlite to two parts soil.

Take care
Give this species a cold winter rest.

☐ Full sun
☐ Temp: 5-30°C (41-86°F)
☐ Keep dry in winter

Echinopsis aurea
SEA-URCHIN CACTUS

Echinopsis aurea is still sometimes listed in catalogues under its old name of *Lobivia aurea,* which can be confusing. The plant has a cylindrical stem about 10cm (4in) high, which is ribbed, the ribs carrying short spines. A few offsets are formed on the main stem, and these may be removed and potted up.

The flowers are a beautiful lemon-yellow, which is an uncommon colour for an echinopsis. The main flush of flowers is in late spring, but odd flowers appear in summer.

Echinopsis plants need to be treated generously. Grow in loam-based mixture, which should be renewed annually. When buds appear, water once every two weeks with a liquid feed, the high-potassium type used for tomatoes. Like most desert cacti, *E. aurea* needs full sunlight to stimulate bud formation. Strong light also results in stout, well-coloured spines.

Take care
Feed generously when in bud, and during flowering.

☐ Full sun
☐ Temp: 5-30°C (41-86°F)
☐ Keep cool and dry in winter

Echinopsis multiplex
BARREL CACTUS
EASTER-LILY CACTUS
PINK EASTER LILY
SEA-URCHIN CACTUS

The delicate pink flowers of this cactus open during the night and remain open during the following day. The flowers have a long tube about 20cm (8in) long and a sweet lily-like scent.

The genuine *E. multiplex* has long thick spines, but many pink-

Left: Echinopsis aurea produces most of its eye-catching lemon-yellow flowers in late spring, but occasionally blooms continue to appear in mid-summer.

Above: Echinopsis multiplex bears delicate pink, sweetly-scented flowers during early summer. Unfortunately, flowers usually fade away after one or two days.

flowered echinopsis plants sold under this name are very short-spined hybrids, probably with *E. eyriesii.*

  E. multiplex produces a profusion of offsets. To enable the main plant to reach flowering size quickly and to keep the plant within bounds, most of the offsets should be removed.

  Large numbers of flowers are produced in early summer, and the plant should be fed during the flowering period with a tomato fertilizer. Any good potting

mixture, either loam- or peat-based, is suitable for this species. Repot annually. Water freely during spring and summer, allowing the compost to dry out between waterings.

Take care
Watch for mealy bug.

___

□ Full sun
□ Temp: 5-30°C (41-86°F)
□ Keep cool and dry in winter

___

Echinopsis Paramount hybrid 'Orange Glory'
SEA-URCHIN CACTUS

'Orange Glory' is one of the beautiful *Echinopsis* x *Lobivia* hybrids that have been produced in the USA. The flowers are a deep glowing orange, a colour not found in pure echinopsis species. The cactus itself is cylindrical, with many ribs; the ribs carry short spines. A few offsets are produced on young plants; these may be left on the plant if a large specimen is desired, or removed for propagation.

This cactus may be grown in any loam- or peat-based mixture. Repot annually. Water freely during the spring and summer months, when the plant is in vigorous growth, but allow to dry out between waterings. When flower buds form feed every two weeks with a tomato fertilizer.

This is a desert plant and needs to be grown in full sunlight to stimulate bud formation and to encourage the growth of strong, well-covered spines. This plant is tough and resistant to most pests.

Take care
Give plenty of sunshine.

□ Full sun
□ Temp: 5-30°C (41-86°F)
□ Keep cool and dry in winter

Right: Epiphyllum 'Ackermannii' is a beautiful orchid cactus, with large, showy, bell-shaped flowers borne during summer.

Epiphyllum 'Ackermannii'
ORCHID CACTUS

Epiphyllums (also known as Epicacti) are among the most un-cactus-like cacti and are often grown by plant lovers who profess no interest in conventional cacti. Nevertheless, they are true cacti, but living naturally in tropical rain forests rather than in the desert. Plants normally cultivated are hybrids between the various wild species and other cacti; such plants are hardier and have more colourful flowers. 'Ackermannii' is a typical example and is one of the oldest in cultivation, but its flowers have not been surpassed in beauty

of colour. They are about 8cm (3.2in) across and brilliant red, but not perfumed. The blooms appear along the notched edges of the stems and may last for several days.

You can grow epiphyllums in a standard houseplant mixture, but if you add extra peat or leaf mould to it, this is beneficial. Also, good drainage is important.

Take care
Feed with high-potassium fertilizer when in bud and flower.

- □ Partial shade
- □ Temp: 5-27°C (41-81°F)
- □ Keep almost dry in winter

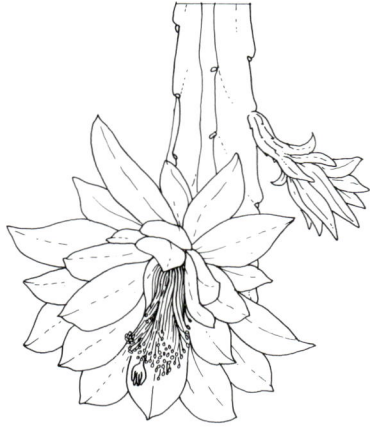

Epiphyllum 'Cooperi'
ORCHID CACTUS

The white flowers of this hybrid epiphyllum are perfumed; quite unusual for a cactus! Unlike those of other similar cacti, the flowers come from the base of the plant, not along the side of the stem. When the large buds are fully formed in spring or summer, they will open in the evening, and if they are in the living-room, a strong lily-like perfume will pervade the whole room at about 10pm. One can almost watch the buds unfold, to give brilliant white blooms maybe 10cm (4in) across.

This cactus will survive at the lower temperature in winter, but will do better if rather warmer. This is easy indoors, in a shady window. Water freely in spring and summer, and keep moister indoors in winter than in a greenhouse. But it appreciates a moist atmosphere; an occasional spray with water will help. Use a good standard potting mixture and feed occasionally.

Take care
Too much nitrogen in feed can cause brown spots.

- □ Partial shade
- □ Temp: 5-27°C (41-81°F)
- □ Keep almost dry in winter

Gymnocalycium bruchii
CHIN CACTUS

A small-growing cactus, and if one had to choose a single beauty, easily obtainable, from among a lovely group, this could well be it. But it has a confusing alias; it is sometimes called *G. lafaldense,* so take care not to buy the same plant twice! A small compact clump of neatly spined, rounded heads is soon formed, which produces pinkish blooms very freely. Far better to leave this cactus as a clump, but often the heads become so crowded that a few can be removed to make room for the others. Carefully cut them away with a thin knife, allow them to dry off for a few days and just press them into fresh potting mix in late spring and summer.

Either loam- or peat-based potting mixture may be used, but increase the drainage by mixing in about one third of sharp sand or perlite. Watering can be quite free in spring and summer, and every two weeks or so give a dose of fertilizer.

Take care
Mealy bugs hide between heads.

□ Full sun
□ Temp: 5-30°C (41-86°F)
□ Keep dry in winter

Above: Gymnocalycium bruchii is a small, compact cactus that soon forms a freely-flowering clump. It is sometimes sold as Gymnocalycium lafaldense.

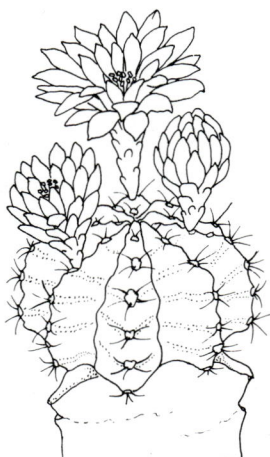

Gymnocalycium mihanovichii 'Hibotan'
CHIN CACTUS
PLAIN CACTUS

Above: Gymnocalycium mihanovichii 'Hibotan' should be grown on a graft, as it contains no food-making chlorophyll.

Below: Hamatocactus setispinus develops yellow flowers with reddish-orange centres. The blooms appear amid the spines.

L ooking something like a tomato on a stick, this cactus, sometimes also called 'ruby ball', is certainly unusual. It was first developed in Japan. Some cacti suppliers incorrectly call it the 'everlasting flower'. But the top is no flower, simply an abnormal version of *G. mihanovichii,* lacking chlorophyll. Consequently this novel cactus must always be grown grafted.

A tender jungle cactus, hylocereus, identified by its three-cornered stem, is most often used as a grafting stock; unless you can keep a winter temperature of at least 10°C (50°F), it is better to re-graft onto something tougher, such as a trichocereus. Otherwise treat 'Hibotan' as a houseplant, for which it is ideally suited. You may be rewarded with attractive white or pink flowers. Use a potting mixture of three parts of a standard material and one part of sharp sand or perlite, and be careful never to overwater.

Take care
Avoid full summer sun.

☐ Partial shade
☐ Temp: 10-30°C (50-86°F)
☐ Keep dryish in winter

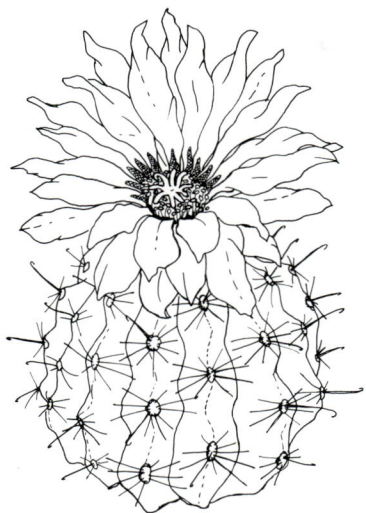

Hamatocactus setispinus

This small cactus does particularly well in cultivation; plants only 2.5cm (1in) across will flower. The yellow blooms have a deep red throat and are borne on the top of the plant during summer. An adult plant is about 13cm (5in) across, with a dark green skin and white spines.

A suitable growing medium for this plant is two parts loam- or peat-based mixture to one part of sharp sand or perlite. Repot annually and inspect the roots for the grey ashy deposits that indicate the presence of root mealy bug. If found, wash the old soil off the roots and repot into a clean container. The plant should be watered freely during the summer months but allowed to dry out between waterings; keep it dry during the winter. Full sun is necessary to stimulate flowering and to encourage the growth of long stout spines. Feed every two weeks with a high-potassium fertilizer when flower buds start to appear.

Take care
Make sure drips in the greenhouse do not spoil winter dryness.

☐ Full sun
☐ Temp: 5-30°C (41-86°F)
☐ Water freely during summer

Lobivia hertrichiana
COB CACTUS

One of the most popular and widely grown of the lobivias, this small cactus flowers very freely, even when quite young. Stems are more or less globular, ribbed, with fairly short, bristly, spreading spines. Individual heads are about 2.5-4cm (1-1.6in) thick, and the plant rapidly forms quite a large clump. But there is no need to let it become any larger than required; heads are easily removed for propagation in spring. Merely let them dry for a few days before potting up. Brilliant scarlet flowers, produced in masses in spring and summer, may be up to 5cm (2in) across.

To get the best from this attractive cactus, let it form a reasonably large clump if space permits, preferably growing it in a pan or half-pot. Use a good standard potting mixture but make sure that it is well drained. A cold winter rest is desirable to promote good flowering, as is feeding in spring and summer.

Take care
A top dressing of gravel will protect the clump from excess water.

□ Full sun
□ Temp: 5-30°C (41-86°F)
□ Keep dry in winter

Above: Lobivia hertrichiana blooms quite freely, even when young. Masses of bright scarlet flowers, up to 5cm (2in) wide, appear in spring and summer.

Below: A many-headed plant, Mammillaria bocasana is mainly grown for its blue-green body and silky spines. Beware: spines are hooked and adhere to clothing.

Mammillaria bocasana
FISH-HOOKS CACTUS
POWDER-PUFF CACTUS
SNOWBALL CACTUS

Mammillarias are the most popular of the cacti: they are small, flower freely, and have beautiful spines. *M. bocasana* is a many-headed plant that forms a cushion. The plant is blue-green and covered with silky white spines. Appearances are deceptive: underneath the soft spines are spines with hooks, which cling to the hands, clothing or anything else that touches them. The small creamy flowers form circlets around each head in spring. This is a very free-flowering plant.

This cactus needs a sunny position and ample water plus a dose of high-potassium (tomato-type) fertilizer every two weeks or so during the growing period. During winter, keep it dry. A suitable mixture is two parts of a loam-based potting medium to one part of sharp sand or perlite. Repot annually. If the plant is becoming too large, remove one of the heads, dry it for two days, and then pot it up. If the cutting is taken in spring, it will soon root.

Take care
Avoid the hooked spines.

□ Full sun
□ Temp: 5-30°C (41-86°F)
□ Keep dry in winter

Above: Mammillaria elongata develops flowers in early spring amid clusters of finger-like stems attractively peppered with variously-coloured spines.

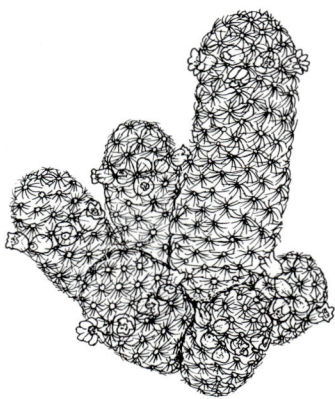

Mammillaria elongata

GOLD LACE CACTUS
GOLDEN-LACE CACTUS
GOLDEN-STAR CACTUS
LACE CACTUS
LADY FINGER CACTUS

M*ammillaria elongata* is a clustering plant that consists of long finger-shaped shoots. The spines are prettily arranged in a star, and are variable in colour; plants exist with white, yellow, brown or deep red spines. The cream flowers are freely produced,

even on small plants, in the early months of spring.

This cactus needs an open mixture, two parts loam- or peat-based potting medium to one part grit. It looks at its best if grown in a half-pot. If the cluster becomes too large, remove a shoot, dry it for two or three days, and pot it up separately. The late spring is a good time to take cuttings. The plant may be watered generously during summer, but keep it dry during winter. Feed every two weeks with a high-potassium fertilizer during the flowering period. Full sunlight is necessary to maintain the rich colour of the spines.

Take care
To avoid weak spines, grow in good sunlight.

□ Full sun
□ Temp: 5-30°C (41-86°F)
□ Keep dry in winter

Mammillaria zeilmanniana
ROSE-PINCUSHION

This is a very free-flowering mammillaria and the blooms are a beautiful reddish-violet colour; it is one of the few mammillarias of this colour to flower as a young plant. Occasionally a plant has flowers

Below: Mammillaria zeilmanniana is one of the most free-flowering and dainty of all mammillarias. It produces a complete ring of blooms.

with a double row of petals, and there is also a form with white blooms. The flowering period is early summer.

The stems of this plant are cylindrical, and branch to form multi-headed clumps. Heads can be detached during summer, and used to propagate the plant. Grow in half-pots; a suitable potting mixture is two parts loam- or peat-based medium and one part grit. Water freely and feed every two weeks with a high-potassium fertilizer during spring and summer, allowing it to dry out between waterings. Let it become almost dry during winter. Keep in a sunny part of the greenhouse and inspect for mealy bug; water with insecticide.

Take care
Do not allow water to accumulate between the heads.

☐ Full sun
☐ Temp: 5-30°C (41-86°F)
☐ Keep almost dry in winter

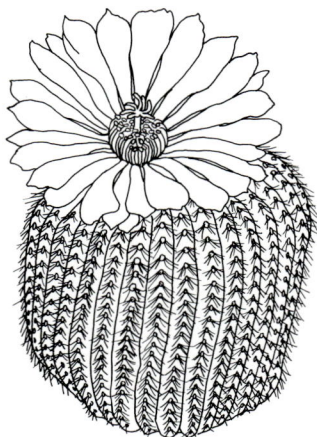

Notocactus leninghausii
BALL CACTUS
GOLDEN BALL CACTUS

Notocactus leninghausii is a golden plant that branches and becomes columnar with age. The many close ribs carry soft yellow spines. It is characteristic that the growing centre of this plant tends to be on one side of the stem. The large yellow flowers appear on top of the plant in late summer. Young plants do not flower.

This cactus is not difficult to cultivate; a growing medium consisting of two parts peat-based potting mixture to one part grit, and a sunny position, will ensure a healthy plant. Repot annually. If the plant gets too large or the base of the stem becomes corky, branches may be removed in summer and used for propagation. Water freely during summer, allowing it to dry out between waterings. During flowering, feed every two weeks with a high-potassium fertilizer. Gradually taper the water off in autumn and keep the plant dry during the winter. Watch out for root mealy bug and mealy bug.

Take care
Avoid damp winter conditions.

□ Full sun
□ Temp: 5-30°C (41-86°F)
□ Keep dry in winter

Right: Notocactus leninghausii is mainly grown for its golden spines rather than for the flowers, which are produced only on older plants.

Notocactus ottonis
BALL CACTUS

Notocactus ottonis is quite different from other notocacti; it is much smaller, and clusters freely from the base. It is deep green, and the ribs carry slender yellowish spines. Individual heads are about 7.5cm (3in) across. The yellow flowers are about 6cm (2.4in) across.

This notocactus is touchy about watering; to prevent it losing its roots, grow in an open mixture consisting of one part loam-based potting medium to one part grit. Grow it in a half-pot: the cluster looks better, and the roots are not surrounded by large quantities of cold, damp soil. Water freely during spring and summer, always allowing it to dry out between waterings. Feed every two weeks during the flowering period using a high-potassium (tomato) fertilizer. Keep it dry in winter. Place this plant where it will get plenty of light. The main pests are mealy bug and root mealy bug; treat with a proprietary insecticide.

Take care
Avoid damp winter conditions.

□ Full sun
□ Temp: 5-30°C (41-86°F)
□ Never overwater

Left: Notocactus ottonis is a small, globular cactus which produces large, brilliant yellow flowers with red centres from early to mid-summer.

Below: Like all other opuntias, Opuntia basilaris is known as a prickly pear. Also called the beaver-tail cactus, it is one of the opuntias which flowers when small, about 20cm (8in) high.

Opuntia basilaris

BEAVER-TAIL CACTUS
CHOLLA CACTUS
PRICKLY PEAR
ROSE TUNA

If there is any typical cactus, it must surely be the opuntia, or prickly pear, although the latter name was originally applied to the spiny fruit of a desert giant. But O. basilaris is not a giant and is ideal for the collection as it rarely becomes more than two segments, or pads, high, sometimes branching from the base. The pads are flattened stems (beaver-tail shape), and although almost spineless, they are dotted with clusters of dark red barbed bristles (glochids), characteristic of all opuntias, spined or not. Most opuntias do not flower readily in a collection, needing to be very large before they do so. But this one, being smaller, will often produce red blooms up to 5cm (2in) across on its second segment, when about 20cm (8in) high.

Grow this opuntia in a good porous potting mixture; extra drainage material is probably not necessary. If you winter it indoors, give just enough water to prevent shrivelling. Best kept dry if in a greenhouse.

Take care
Glochids can penetrate skin.

□ Full sun
□ Temp: 5-30°C (41-86°F)
□ Keep dry in winter

Opuntia microdasys

BUNNY-EARS
CHOLLA CACTUS
GOLDPLUSH
PRICKLY PEAR
RABBIT-EARS
YELLOW BUNNY-EARS

Probably the most common cactus of all, and certainly the most popular opuntia; but also the most ill-treated cactus. Witness the poor, spotted, dried-up plants so common in windows. Although it spreads over a wide area in the wild, cultivated specimens form small branched bushes, consisting of many beautiful bright green pads, or flattened stem segments, closely dotted with clumps of yellow glochids (barbed bristles) but no other spines. There are also varieties with reddish and white glochids. All are beautiful but need careful handling, because the pads are not as innocent as they look; the glochids stick into the skin at the slightest opportunity. Rarely, yellow flowers are produced.

A well-drained potting mixture is needed, and free watering in spring and summer. Give sufficient water in winter to prevent undue shrivelling and keep this cactus rather warmer than it would be in the average cool greenhouse.

Take care
Cold winter conditions cause brown spots.

□ Full sun
□ Temp: 10-30°C (50-86°F)
□ Keep slightly moist in winter

Below: A slow-growing cactus, Opuntia microdasys is mainly grown for its beautiful pads. There are several varieties.

Above: Opuntia robusta is a natural giant, but small specimens are attractive in a collection. However, small plants are not likely to produce flowers.

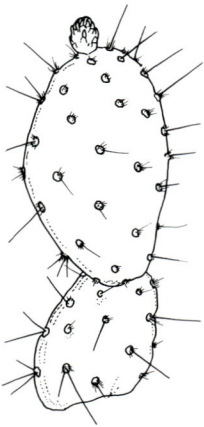

Opuntia robusta
CHOLLA CACTUS
PRICKLY PEAR

Although this cactus is one of the giant opuntias in its native state, where it can reach a height of 5m (16ft) with bluish-green pads the size of dinner plates, it can be tamed as a pot plant and makes a good, tough specimen for the average collection. This species grows quite quickly for a cactus, and soon makes a nice plant, but without the glorious yellow flowers of desert specimens, as you will not want it to get large enough for that!

It is easy to prevent it from becoming too big: just remove one or more pads when there is any danger of this, let them dry for a few days, and start another specimen. The old plant will send out further shoots, if you want them; otherwise, throw it away! Living up to its name, *O. robusta* is hardy enough to be grown out of doors throughout the year, if it can be protected from winter rain, but it must be dry to survive. Ordinary, good potting mixture will suffice.

Take care
Protect from slugs outdoors.

□ Full sun
□ Temp: 0-30°C (32-86°F)
□ Keep dry in winter

Grow this particularly easy opuntia in any good standard potting mixture and it should delight you every summer with its show of snow-white flowers, up to 4cm (1.6in) across, freely produced along the stems. The long, slender stems will need staking, or supporting in some way; a miniature pot plant trellis is ideal and the stems can be gently tied to this. Water freely in spring and summer; plants indoors may need a little water in winter to prevent shedding.

Take care
Handle gently.

Opuntia salmiana
CHOLLA CACTUS
PRICKLY PEAR

☐ Full sun
☐ Temp: 5-30°C (41-86°F)
☐ Keep dry in winter

There should be no trouble whatsoever in flowering this opuntia, even in a 5cm (2in) pot. It is quite different from the others mentioned: it does not have flattened 'pads' but long, slender cylindrical stems, freely branching; which in pot-grown specimens usually reach a length of about 30cm (12in) with a thickness of only 1cm (0.4in). Patches of barbed bristles (glochids) and very short spines are distributed over the stems. Large or small branches drop off at the slightest touch, usually rooting where they fall.

Below: Opuntia salmiana is one of the cylindrical-jointed opuntias, which are less familiar than the 'prickly pear' shaped ones. Its outstanding characteristic is that it can be expected to flower easily in a small pot, which is unlikely in the case of the larger-growing opuntias. The cylindrical stems tend to trail, and this cactus needs to be supported in some way, possibly on a plastic trellis as used for houseplants. Otherwise, it could be planted in a hanging basket, but be careful that it does not get tangled in anyone's hair!

Opuntia scheerii
CHOLLA CACTUS
PRICKLY PEAR

By contrast with certain other opuntias, this one is ideal for the collection without any size-reducing manipulations. The flattened pads or stem segments are usually around 15cm (6in) long and 5cm (2in) broad, but older plants produce larger ones. A decorative, bushy plant results from branches off the main segment. The whole surface of each pad is covered with a network of golden spines, in addition to the inevitable barbed bristles (glochids). Flowers are yellow, but unlikely in cultivation.

Grow this cactus in a standard potting mixture, either peat- or loam-based, preferably with the addition of one third of sharp sand or perlite. Slight shrivelling of the stems may occur if the plant is quite dry in winter, as it should be if in a cool greenhouse; but in a warmer room give it just enough water to prevent this happening. You can water quite freely in spring and summer. Pads can be removed for propagation.

Take care
Mealy bugs tend to collect at the base of joints.

□ Full sun
□ Temp: 5-30°C (41-86°F)
□ Keep dry in winter

Above: Opuntia scheerii has the typical glochids (barbed bristles) of an opuntia, as well as a network of golden spines covering the joints. With its compact habit of growth and flat pads or segments, it is ideal for the average collection, and it is unlikely to become too large for many years. If and when it does, it is a simple matter to re-start by removing a few joints and treating them as cuttings. They can be potted up after a few days' drying to seal the cut surface. The best time to do this is late spring to summer.

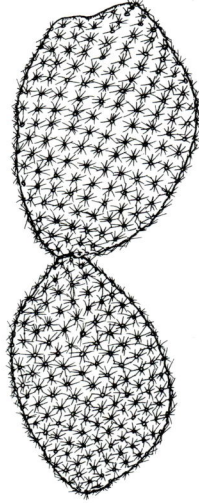

Pereskia aculeata

With this plant you will have difficulty in persuading your friends that it is a cactus at all. Pereskias are the most un-cactus-like of all cacti, but their spine formation and flower structure prove their identity. This plant is scarcely succulent at all; with its large privet-like leaves and slightly spiny long trailing stems, it somewhat resembles a wild rose. The leaves are bright green, but the variety *godseffiana* (often called *Pereskia godseffiana*) has reddish tinged leaves. The stems will need supporting in some way, with sticks or a plant trellis. In a greenhouse it can be trained up and along the roof, but the rather higher winter temperature needed makes it difficult for the cool greenhouse. Indoors, it should thrive in a light window, large enough to accommodate its stems.

Pinkish flowers, rather like those of a wild rose and about 4.5cm (1.8in) across, appear in autumn, but only on large plants. Water freely in spring and summer and feed occasionally.

Take care
Cold conditions cause leaf fall.

□ Full sun
□ Temp: 10-30°C (50-86°F)
□ Keep slightly moist in winter

Right: Pereskia aculeata is a strange cactus, with flowers almost like those of a wild rose. It needs some support.

Rebutia albiflora
CROWN CACTUS

Rebutia albiflora is one of the very few rebutias with white flowers. This is a very desirable plant if space is limited; it will flower when only 1cm (0.4in) across. The flowering period is spring. The plant consists of a cluster of small heads, covered in short white spines. Individual heads can be split off and used to start new plants.

This cactus has a weak root system and should be grown in a shallow pan so that the roots are not surrounded by large quantities of cold, wet soil. A loam-based mixture or a soilless medium, to which one third sharp sand or perlite has been added, is suitable for this cactus. During spring and summer water freely, allowing it to dry out between waterings. Feed every two weeks with a tomato fertilizer when the buds appear. During the winter months keep it dry.

Mealy bug and root mealy bug are the pests most likely to attack this rebutia. A proprietary insecticide spray will deal with these.

Take care
Do not overwater.

□ Full sun
□ Temp: 5-30°C (41-86°F)
□ Water with care

Rebutia calliantha var. krainziana

All rebutias are beautiful in the spring flowering period, but this species is outstanding. Each head is surrounded by a complete ring of orange-red flowers. The flower colour in this plant can vary from an almost true red through to a pure orange. The buds are purple.

The individual heads of this clustering cactus are cylindrical, and reach a height of about 10cm (4in). The very short white spines form a neat pattern against the green stem.

This rebutia needs a sunny position to keep it a bright colour and to ensure flowering. Any good potting mixture may be used, either loam- or peat-based. During spring and summer water freely, letting it get almost dry before watering again. When the buds form feed every two weeks with a tomato fertilizer.

Watch carefully for any signs of mealy bug, particularly around the growing point of the stems, where these woolly white pests can fade into the white wool on new growth.

Take care
Give plenty of light.

□ Full sun
□ Temp: 5-30°C (41-86°F)
□ Avoid overwatering

Above: Rebutia calliantha var. krainziana is a small cactus, ideal for a collection on a windowsill. Its beautiful, orange-red flowers appear in spring.

Left: Rebutia albiflora is one of the smallest rebutias, revealing clustered heads and an all-white appearance, with white spines and unusual white flowers.

Rebutia senilis
FIRE-CROWN CACTUS

Rebutias are ideal cacti for the collector without a greenhouse. They are small and will flower freely every spring if kept on a sunny windowsill. One of the prettiest is *R. senilis:* the rings of red flowers show up well against the silvery white spines. The flowers are followed by seed pods, and in autumn dozens of seedling rebutias will be found nestling around the parent plant. With age *R. senilis* clusters, forming a cushion about 30cm (12in) across. Individual heads may be removed and used for propagation.

Rebutias are not fussy about their soil, and either a loam-based or a soilless mixture may be used. In spring and summer water freely, allowing the compost to dry out between waterings. When the buds form feed every two weeks with a high-potassium fertilizer.

Carefully watch for signs of mealy bug. It is easy to miss these white pests on a white-spined plant. A systemic insecticide will be ideal.

Take care
Check for mealy bug.

- ☐ Full sun
- ☐ Temp: 5-30°C (41-86°F)
- ☐ Water with care

Right: Schlumbergera 'Buckleyi' is a popular cactus, with eye-catching flowers. This is one of several hybrids now available.

Below: Rebutia senilis creates a wealth of red flowers in spring amid silvery-white spines. It belongs to a genus which is one of the most floriferous of all cacti.

Schlumbergera 'Buckleyi'
CHRISTMAS CACTUS

There is no doubt that this is the most popular cactus of all and the one most commonly grown, in spite of the fact that many people do not consider it to be a 'true' cactus. But it *is* a cactus, a jungle type, needing more warmth and moisture than the desert cacti. The many segments, joined end to end, are true stems (there are no leaves) and the whole plant forms a densely branched bush. Unscented flowers of an unusual shape and about 3cm (1.2in) across, are freely produced in winter. They bloom from the end of segments; the typical colour is carmine but varieties exist with flowers of various shades of red, pink or even white (never blue).

Use a rich potting mixture with added peat or leaf mould, and water the plant freely when in bud and flower, feeding every two weeks at this time. Reduce the water somewhat after flowering. Propagation from segments is easy.

Take care
Buds drop if the plant is moved.

☐ Partial shade
☐ Temp: 10-30°C (50-86°F)
☐ Keep slightly moist all year

Trichocereus chilensis

Trichocerei are pretty when small, but this cactus will not grow too large during the lifetime of its owner. If you see this one offered for sale it is well worth acquiring. With naturally large-growing cacti it is difficult to state a definite size but a good cultivated specimen would be about 20cm (8in) high and 5-8cm (2-3.2in) across after many years. But you are likely to buy this one at around 5cm (2in) high. The long golden-brown, stout spines arranged along the many-ribbed bright green stems make this a most attractive cactus, which is just as well, because it is of no use to expect flowers except on very large specimens. But the white flowers, when produced, are beautiful and pleasantly perfumed. Because the stem is unbranched, propagation from cuttings is not possible.

Any good standard peat- or loam-based potting mixture will do for this very tolerant cactus and you can water it freely in spring and summer.

Take care
The spines are needle-sharp!

☐ Full sun
☐ Temp: 5-30°C (41-86°F)
☐ Keep dry in winter

Right: Trichocereus spachianus is an ideal cactus for a windowsill, where its beautiful greenish-white flowers appear at night.

Trichocereus spachianus
GOLDEN COLUMN
TORCH CACTUS
WHITE TORCH CACTUS

This trichocereus is a naturally large cactus that makes a good smaller specimen for a collection. It could easily reach a height of 30cm (12in), with bright green stems eventually branching from the base. The blunt ribs bear only quite short spines, and the plant is reasonably easy to handle. If allowed to become large enough it may well respond by producing large greenish-white flowers from the top, opening at night. But the main use for this plant is as a grafting stock for other cacti, and unless you want a large specimen, it is simplicity itself to produce many small ones. If any branch is cut off, not only will it root if given the usual few days' drying-off period, but the stump will send out a ring of offsets, which can be removed and potted up in their turn.

With a good standard porous potting mixture, peat- or loam-based, it is not necessary to add extra drainage material. Water freely in spring and summer.

Take care
Tall plants become top-heavy.

□ Full sun
□ Temp: 5-30°C (41-86°F)
□ Keep dry in winter

Moderately Easy to Grow

The cacti featured in this section require a little more attention than those on the previous pages — for example, some need watering with great care, especially in winter — but nonetheless they are relatively easy to grow even in the smallest house.

It is interesting to note that not all plants from the same genus require the same degree of care in their cultivation. For that reason you should ensure that you buy the right species for the skills you have acquired. For instance, *Mammillaria bombycina* (featured in this section) is easier to grow than *Mammillaria perbella* (featured in the 'Difficult to Grow' section). Occasionally, however, it is worth getting one or two plants that are slightly more difficult as they broaden your experience and create a fresh challenge.

waterings and if possible water on a sunny day. Feed every two weeks with a high-potassium (tomato) fertilizer when the buds form. If it should lose its roots, allow the plant to dry for two or three days and repot in fresh, well-drained mixture. Keep in a well-lit position.

Take care
Water sparingly.

- Full sun
- Temp: 5-30°C (41-86°F)
- Water with care

Acanthocalycium violaceum
VIOLET SEA-URCHIN

Acanthocalycium violaceum is a cylindrical plant about 12cm (4.7in) in diameter. During summer, it produces large numbers of beautiful violet flowers, about 5cm (2in) across. Even during winter the plant is attractive, and the stout yellow spines show up well against the dark green of the stem. This cactus does not offset easily, certainly not as a young plant; many apparently solitary plants do occasionally form offsets with age.

A good potting mixture is two parts of loam- or peat-based material to one part of sharp sand or perlite. *A. violaceum* should be watered with caution even during the summer growing period. Always allow it to dry out between

Above: Astrophytum myriostigma has a distinctive shape, as well as attractive flowers during summer. It needs as much light as possible, so place it on a bright windowsill.

Astrophytum myriostigma
BISHOP'S-CAP CACTUS
BISHOP'S-HOOD
BISHOP'S MITRE
MONKSHOOD

*A*strophytum myriostigma is a cylindrical plant eventually reaching a diameter of 20cm (8in). The dark green skin is completely covered with silvery scales. The number of ribs varies from four to eight. They are spineless, but the

Left: Acanthocalycium violaceum is an attractive, globular-shaped cactus. Initially, the spines are yellow, later turning brown and rather less attractive.

prominent areoles give the plant the appearance of having been buttoned into its skin. The flowers appear on the top of the plant continuously throughout the summer. They are yellow with a sweet scent.

This is the easiest of the astrophytums to grow. A loam-based or peat-based mixture plus one third extra grit is suitable. Water freely throughout the summer, giving a liquid tomato fertilizer every two weeks, but keep dry in winter. This cactus is a native of the Mexican deserts and in cultivation needs the maximum light available. Mealy bug and root mealy bug can be a nuisance. Small white mealy bugs look very much like white scales.

Take care
Allow to dry between waterings.

□ Full sun
□ Temp: 5-30°C (41-86°F)
□ Dry winter rest

53

Left: A spiny cactus, Astrophytum ornatum needs to be fairly large before forming flowers — usually after ten or more years.

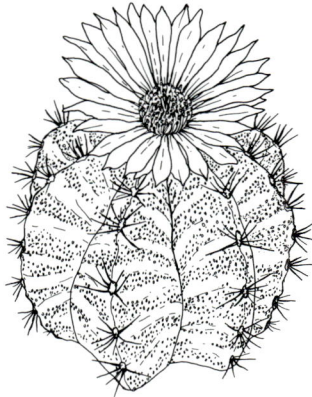

Astrophytum ornatum
BISHOP'S-CAP
ORNAMENTAL MONKSHOOD
STAR CACTUS

*A*strophytum ornatum does not bloom until it is about 15cm (6in) high, and it will probably take about 10 years to reach flowering size. But even without flowers, this is an attractive cactus. The stem is divided by eight ribs, which carry stout amber-coloured spines. The dark green skin has bands of silvery scales running across it. The attractive yellow flowers are carried on top of the plant and are sweetly scented.

To keep the superb colouring of this cactus, it needs sun. A useful mix is two parts loam- or peat-based medium plus one part sharp sand or perlite. Water generously throughout the summer, allowing to dry out before watering again. When the buds form give a dose of tomato fertilizer every two weeks. Keep the soil dry throughout the winter. Repot the plant annually, and inspect the roots for any grey ashy deposits, a sign that root mealy bug is present; if it is, water with an insecticide.

Take care
Make sure drips in the greenhouse do not spoil winter dryness.

□ Full sun
□ Temp: 5-30°C (41-86°F)
□ Water with care

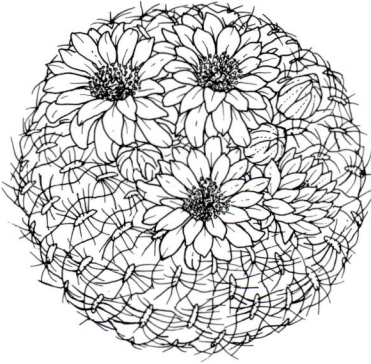

Borzicactus aureiflora
(Matucana aureiflora)

The two names given for this cactus indicate that it also has been subjected to re-classification and it is more likely that you will meet it under *Matucana.* Although in nature the globular stem can reach a diameter of 30cm (12in), specimens in cultivation are likely to be much smaller, with a flattened rather than a globular stem. A number of blunt ribs carry colourful, stout spreading spines.

Bright yellow flowers, usually about 3cm (1.2in) across, are formed at the top of the stem in summer.

Use a porous potting mixture, which you can make by adding about one third of sharp sand or perlite to a standard loam- or peat-based material. Water this cactus quite freely in summer and feed once every two weeks or so with a high-potassium fertilizer, such as is given to tomatoes. Really good light will help to develop the fine spine coloration; give it full sunlight if at all possible.

Take care
If in a room, put it in the sunniest window.

□ Full sun
□ Temp: 5-30°C (41-86°F)
□ Keep dry in winter

Below: Borzicactus aureiflora produces a mass of bright yellow flowers at the top of its body during summer. Place on a sunny windowsill, in good light.

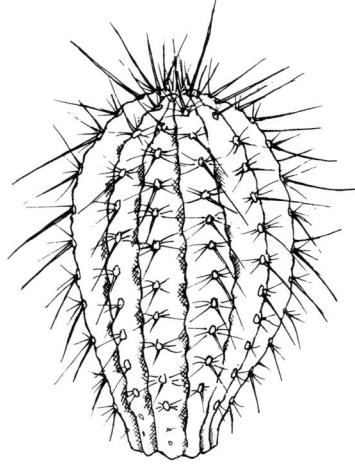

Carnegiea gigantea
ARIZONA GIANT
GIANT CACTUS
GIANT SAGUARO
SAGUARO

Symbolic of many Western films and also used as the state sign of Arizona, this is one of the largest cacti, but because it is very slow-growing it is quite suitable as a pot plant. Although in nature it can reach a height of 15m (50ft), it takes about 200 years to do so; hardly likely to inconvenience the collector! An average domestic specimen would be about 15cm (6in) high in ten years. It forms a green, ribbed column with short spines, and will not produce the up-pointing arms characteristic of giant desert plants; it is unlikely to flower in the owner's lifetime. Although not particularly spectacular as a potted cactus, it is nevertheless of interest because of its association with the desert giants.

Grow *C. gigantea* in a particularly well-drained potting mixture; add one part of sharp sand or perlite to two parts of a good standard loam- or peat-based material. A top dressing of gravel 1cm (0.4in) thick will help to avoid rotting at the base.

Take care
Never overwater this cactus.

Above: Carnegiea gigantea is a hallmark of many Western films, but in a pot it seldom exceeds 15-23cm (6-9in) high and is too small to develop flowers.

☐ Full sun
☐ Temp: 5-30°C (41-86°F)
☐ Keep dry in winter

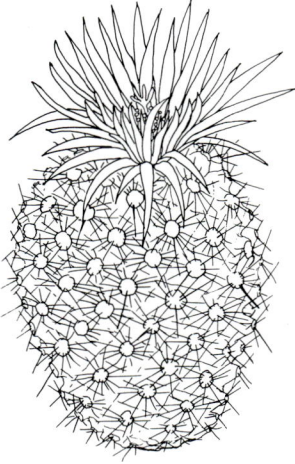

Coryphantha vivipara

Coryphanthas are small, globular cacti, very suitable for collectors with limited space. *C. vivipara* is a freely clustering plant; it is grey in colour and the stem is divided into tubercles. The tips of the tubercles carry white spines. The reddish flowers are borne on the top of the plant during the summer. The plant may be left as a cluster or some offsets used for propagation.

Any good potting mixture, either loam- or peat-based, may be used, with about one third of extra grit. During the late spring and summer, water freely, allowing the soil to dry out between waterings. Feed every two weeks with a high-potassium fertilizer when the buds form. Keep it dry in the winter. A sunny position is needed, because strong light stimulates bud formation and keeps the spines a good colour.

Mealy bug and root mealy bug are the pests most likely to be found; if so, water with a proprietary insecticide. If root mealy bugs are discovered, wash all the old soil off the roots and scrub the pot.

Take care
Do not let the soil get soggy.

□ Full sun
□ Temp: 5-30°C (41-86°F)
□ Water carefully

Echinocereus perbellus

One of the so-called 'pectinate' echinocerei, this shows a completely different type of stem from the more prostrate species. Here we have a predominantly solitary cactus, which may nevertheless form a low cluster with age. The stem is at first almost spherical and about 5cm (2in) across, but may eventually become more elongated. This stem is beautiful in itself; its many small ribs, closely decorated with short spreading spines ('pectinate', or 'comb-like'), give a delightful, clean, neat appearance. The deep pink to purple flowers add to the attraction: about 5cm (2in) across, they open from hairy buds.

This cactus is almost completely hardy and can withstand dry freezing conditions in winter; but, to be on the safe side, keep to the recommended temperature, if possible. Grow it in a standard potting mixture to which has been added about one third of sharp sand or perlite.

Take care
Mealy bugs may hide among the spreading spines.

□ Full sun
□ Temp: 5-30°C (41-86°F)
□ Keep dry in winter

Left: A free-flowering small cactus, Coryphantha vivipara usually forms a clump of globular stems. With well-drained compost it can survive low temperatures.

Above: Echinocereus perbellus is a small, globular cactus with a distinctive spine formation. Large flowers are produced even on quite young plants.

*Above: Ferocactus acanthodes has
a ferocious appearance, with
sharp, vicious spines. It is slow-
growing and ideal in a collection.
Take care when watering it.*

Ferocactus acanthodes
BARREL CACTUS
FISH-HOOK CACTUS

'Ferocactus' means 'ferocious
cactus' and this aptly describes
these plants, with their array of
sharp, tough spines. *F. acanthodes*
is a particularly attractive member
of the group. It is spherical,
becoming more elongated with
age, and the many ribs are
furnished with reddish spines up to
4cm (1.6in) long, some of them
curved. A giant cactus in nature, it
is slow-growing and perfectly
suitable as a pot specimen; in a pot
it can attain a diameter of 15cm
(6in) or more, but takes years to do
so. However, small plants do not
usually flower.

Ferocacti are particularly
sensitive to insufficient light and
overwatering, so give this one all
the direct sunshine you can, and
add extra drainage material to a
standard peat- or loam-based
potting mixture (one part to two
parts mixture). It is best to water
only when the mixture has almost
dried out. A top dressing of grit or
gravel will keep the base dry.

Take care
Watch for drips in the greenhouse;
they could be fatal!

□ Full sun
□ Temp: 5-30°C (41-86°F)
□ Keep dry in winter

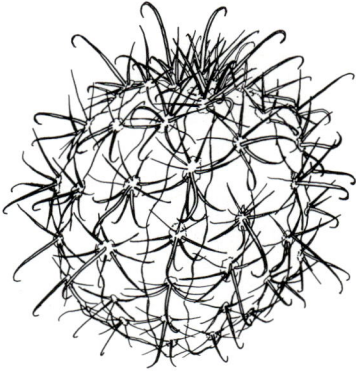

Ferocactus horridus

A fiercely armed cactus with an almost globular stem — which in cultivation is unlikely to exceed a diameter of 10cm (4in) — divided into about 12 ribs. Very strong, reddish spines occur in groups along the ribs, up to 5cm (2in) long; the longest spine in each group is flattened and hooked at the tip. Ideally designed to catch in the clothing and pull the plant off the staging! Although yellow flowers can be produced, they are unlikely on smaller plants, so it is best not to hope for them, but to be content with the plant itself.

Grow this ferocactus in a porous potting mixture, which you can make up by adding one part of sharp sand or perlite to two parts of a standard material, and mixing it thoroughly. It is best to water only on sunny days in summer, to avoid any risk of the potting mixture becoming too wet. If the plant should lose its roots, cut it back to clean tissue and allow to dry out for a few days before replanting.

Take care
To handle, wrap it in a thick fold of newspaper!

□ Full sun
□ Temp: 5-30°C (41-86°F)
□ Keep dry in winter

Below: Ferocactus horridus is another spiny cactus. Only large plants are likely to produce the yellow flowers.

Above: Ferocactus latispinus has wide, sharp and stiff spines. It is quite likely to flower, but only in warm and sunny conditions.

Right: Frailea castanea is a spectacular cactus with bright yellow flowers that bloom in spring and summer.

Ferocactus latispinus
DEVIL'S-TONGUE

Probably the best-known of the ferocacti, and if you want only one from this group, this is the one to choose. Unlike most of the others, which usually need to reach massive proportions before flowering, this is a species that should burst into bloom when it reaches a diameter of about 10cm (4in). The flowers, 4cm (1.6in) across, are a beautiful purple-red in colour, and open in succession from autumn until early winter. But here lies the snag: unless the autumn is warm and sunny, the buds will probably not open at all! The deeply indented ribs of the bright green stem bear rows of strong, deep yellow spines, some flattened and tipped with red; the whole plant when in flower is a magnificent sight.

As with other ferocacti, a well-drained potting mixture is essential; one part of sharp sand or perlite mixed into two parts of a standard material will prevent any risk of waterlogging, often fatal.

Take care
Keep in the sunniest place.

□ Full sun
□ Temp: 5-30°C (41-86°F)
□ Keep dry in winter

Frailea castanea

This one is a real dwarf cactus, a good-sized specimen being only about 4cm (1.6in) across and almost spherical in shape. Formerly known as *F. asteroides,* it is rather like a miniature version of the cactus *Astrophytum asterias* in appearance, though not in size or in colouring, as it is a greyish bronze. The slightly flattened plant body has a number of blunt ribs; the tiny clumps of spines are more a decoration than a menace. This little cactus flowers quite readily in spring and summer but fraileas exhibit an unusual phenomenon in that the flowers are mostly self-pollinated without opening. Occasionally, however, on a really sunny day the flowers open normally; they are yellow.

Grow *Frailea castanea* in a mixture of standard material and sharp sand or perlite in proportions of about three to one. With such a small plant, you are never likely to need a pot larger than 5cm (2in). A top dressing of grit will protect the plant base.

Take care
Very small pots dry out easily.

☐ Full sun
☐ Temp: 5-30°C (41-86°F)
☐ Keep dry in winter

Gymnocalycium andreae
CHIN CACTUS

Most gymnocalyciums are fairly small, compact cacti, very suitable for the average collection, but this one is particularly desirable as it only reaches a diameter of about 5cm (2in), although a small clump is eventually formed. The spines, some of which are curved, are quite short. This little plant is very free-flowering, producing its bright yellow blooms, about 3cm (1.2in) across, in spring and summer. The colour is unusual for a gymnocalycium, which mostly have white or greenish-white flowers. Offsets soon appear on the main plant; they can be removed for propagation, or left on to produce eventually a rounded mass of beautifully flowering heads.

Full sun is needed, and any good potting mixture may be used, either loam-based or loamless. But good drainage is essential and about one third of extra sharp sand or perlite should be added. During late spring and summer water freely but let the plant become almost dry first.

Take care
Watch out for the mealy bug pest.

□ Full sun
□ Temp: 5-30°C (41-86°F)
□ Keep dry in winter

Above: Gymnocalycium andreae is very free-flowering, producing bright yellow blooms in spring and summer. Full sun is essential for the development of flowers.

Gymnocalycium baldianum
CHIN CACTUS

Like *Gymnocalycium andreae*
this cactus is different from the
general run of gymnocalyciums in
the colour of its flowers, in this
case a brilliant red, although pink-
flowered versions are to be found.
It is sometimes met under its
former name of *G. venturianum,*
which may lead to some confusion
when looking through
nurserymen's lists. The stem is a
bright green ball with a diameter of
about 7cm (2.8in) and seldom
produces offsets. The well-rounded
ribs show the typical
gymnocalycium notches or 'chins'.
Well-treated plants produce
beautiful flowers, about 4cm (1.6in)
across, in spring and summer. Like
most cacti, this one will give of its
best in a greenhouse, but there is
no reason why it should not be
grown and flowered on a sunny
windowsill.

   Use a good, well-drained potting
mixture, as for the preceding
species, and feed every two weeks
with a high-potassium fertilizer
during spring and summer.

Take care
Avoid damp and cold conditions.

□ Full sun
□ Temp: 5-30°C (41-86°F)
□ Keep dry in winter

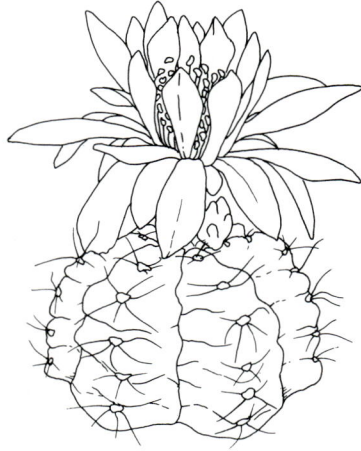

*Below: Gymnocalycium
baldianum creates a mass of
brilliant red flowers during spring
and summer. There are also some
very attractive pink versions.*

The deep green plant body or stem is furnished with broad ribs and the notches along them give the typical 'chin' effect, although this is less pronounced than in other similar plants. The popular name of 'spider cactus' refers to the short spreading spines, somewhat resembling small spiders crawling over the plant. Beautiful greenish-white or pinkish flowers add to the attractiveness of this cactus during spring and summer. They are about 5cm (2in) across.

Grow this cactus in a potting mixture of about two thirds standard growing medium and one third sharp sand or perlite and feed occasionally with a high-potassium fertilizer during the bud and flower stage.

Take care
Make sure the winter dryness is not spoilt by greenhouse drips!

- □ Full sun
- □ Temp: 5-30°C (41-86°F)
- □ Keep dry in winter

Gymnocalycium denudatum
CHIN CACTUS
SPIDER CACTUS

This is perhaps the best-known gymnocalycium and more or less typical of the whole group. It is an almost globular cactus reaching the size of about 15cm (6in) across and 10cm (4in) high.

*Above: Gymnocalycium
horridispinum has outstandingly
attractive satiny-pink flowers. It
needs a cool, dry, winter rest.*

Gymnocalycium
horridispinum
CHIN CACTUS

One of the attractions of
gymnocalyciums is their great
variety of shape, spines and
flowers, and this one is indeed a
beauty among them. It is rather
less typical of the group as a

*Left: Sometimes known as the
'spider cactus', Gymnocalycium
denudatum produces magnificent
flowers in spring and summer.*

whole, being more elongated than
globular; an average-sized plant is
about 13cm (5in) tall and 8cm
(3.2in) broad. Also it has delightful
pink flowers up to 6cm (2.4in)
across. In spite of their size, three
or four flowers can be produced at
a time, and they may last for up to
a week. Unfortunately, they have
no perfume! There are well-formed
'chins' along the ribs of the bright
green stem and these bear stout,
spreading spines, about 3cm (1.2in)
long. Incidentally, its Latin name
does not mean 'horrid', but
'prickly' or 'spiny'.

Grow this lovely plant in the
usual well-drained standard potting
mixture with extra sharp sand or
perlite, and feed occasionally in
spring and summer.

Take care
Avoid soggy potting mixture.

☐ Full sun
☐ Temp: 5-30°C (41-86°F)
☐ Keep dry in winter

Gymnocalycium quehlianum
CHIN CACTUS

Probably the most common gymnocalycium, and one of the hardiest. It is an ideal beginner's cactus. Large, lustrous flowers, up to 6cm (2.4in) across, white with pink centres, are abundantly produced, even on small plants. The plant is a flattened sphere, about 10cm (4in) across and 6cm (2.4in) high when fully grown, with deep rounded ribs and pronounced 'chins'. Offsets are rarely produced and the yellowish, curved spines are quite short. Although individual flowers last for only a day or two, a succession means that this fine cactus is in bloom for several weeks during spring and summer.

Water quite freely from spring until late summer, and use a high-potassium fertilizer about once every two weeks when the plant is in bud and flower. Add about one third of sharp sand or perlite to any good standard peat- or loam-based potting mixture.

Take care
Never let water collect in the depressed top of the plant.

□ Full sun
□ Temp: 2-30°C (36-86°F)
□ Keep dry in winter

Right: A widely-grown cactus, Gymnocalycium quehlianum bears highly attractive lustrous white flowers with pink centres during spring and summer.

Above: Lobivia backebergii has large, brilliant flowers, making it the showpiece of any collection. The almost globular stems are usually solitary, but sometimes offsets are formed at the base. Keep this cactus dry in winter.

Lobivia backebergii
COB CACTUS

The lobivias are a large group of cacti closely related to the genus *Echinopsis,* and many hybrids exist between them. *L. backebergii* starts by being an almost globular plant and gradually becomes more oval. It will not create much of a space problem, as it reaches a diameter of only 5cm (2in). The bright green ribbed stem will sometimes form offsets from the base. Curved spines spread over the ribs, about 1.5cm (0.6in) long, but may be larger if the plant is grown in strong sunlight. The beautiful flowers are carmine with a bluish sheen, and are about 4cm (1.6in) across.

This cactus is quite tolerant with regard to the potting mixture. If your standard mix looks at all compacted, add some extra sharp sand or perlite. Water it freely during spring and summer, and to encourage continued flowering add a high-potassium, tomato-type fertilizer to the water about once every two weeks during this time.

Take care
Good flowering demands a cold winter rest.

□ Full sun
□ Temp: 5-30°C (41-86°F)
□ Keep dry in winter

Flowers are normally yellow, around 5cm (2in) across, and occur in clusters at the top of the stems. Quite often they will open for several days in succession, closing at night. Don't be perturbed if your specimen produces flowers of another colour: there are varieties with orange, pink or red flowers.

This pretty lobivia is rather more moisture- and temperature-sensitive than many, so make sure that the potting mixture is very well drained by adding one part of sharp sand or perlite to three parts of a standard material. Water quite freely on sunny days during spring and summer. Stems can be removed for propagation in spring, but let them dry for a few days before potting.

Take care
Spines can hide mealy bugs.

□ Full sun
□ Temp: 5-30°C (41-86°F)
□ Keep dry in winter

Lobivia densispina
COB CACTUS

A small, particularly beautiful lobivia, this cactus is clump-forming, with individual 'heads' about 6cm (2.4in) long and 2.5cm (1in) thick. The whitish spines on the 20 or so small ribs are so numerous and interlocking that they almost cover the stem.

Above: Mammillaria bombycina comes from a genus which exhibits great variation in shape and spine formation, not to mention the usually freely produced flowers. This species is not one of the best for flowering, at least not in the case of young plants, but its delightful appearance more than compensates, and the flowers are small but beautiful.

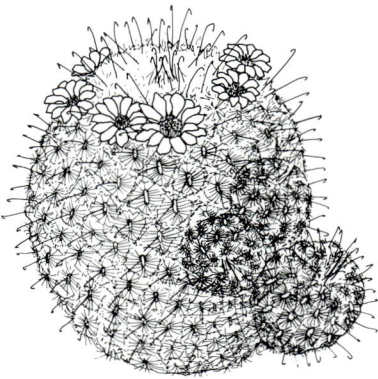

Mammillaria bombycina

Mammillaria bombycina is one of the beautiful white-spined mammillarias. It is initially spherical, later cylindrical, and clump-forming. It is densely covered with spines. The reddish-purple flowers form circlets around the tops of the stems in late spring to early summer. Young plants do not flower. It seems to be characteristic of mammillarias that cream-flowered species bloom easily, even as young plants, but most of the red-flowered ones bloom only as mature plants.

An open growing medium, two parts loam- or peat-based potting mixture to one part grit, is necessary for this cactus. Since it spreads outwards, it looks well grown in a half-pot. Repot annually and examine the roots for signs of root mealy bug. Water generously during summer, but allow it to dry out before watering again. Feed every two weeks with a high-potassium fertilizer when the plant is flowering. Keep dry in winter.

Take care
Avoid a damp, cold atmosphere.

□ Full sun
□ Temp: 5-30°C (41-86°F)
□ Keep dry in winter

Left: Lobivia densispina produces masses of eye-catching red flowers with bright-faced centres. There are also related forms with yellow, orange or pink flowers.

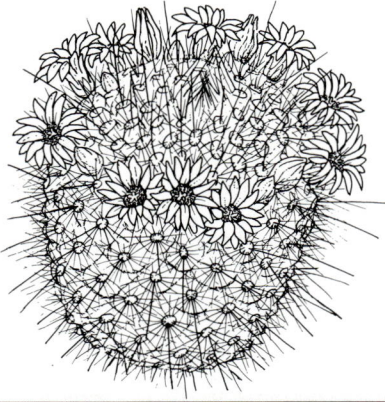

Mammillaria spinosissima

Mammillaria spinosissima comes from Central Mexico and produces large, purplish-pink flowers in rings during summer. Bristle-like red and white spines cover all parts of the plant's dark green body. Several varieties, including 'auricoma', are available.

This cactus is easy to cultivate. A porous mixture consisting of two parts loam- or peat-based material to one part sharp sand or perlite is

needed, and a sunny position. Repot annually. Water generously during spring and summer, but allow it to dry out between waterings. When the flower buds appear, feed every two weeks with a high-potassium (tomato) fertilizer until flowering is over. Keep it dry in late autumn and winter. When repotting, inspect the roots for any ashy deposit, which indicates the presence of root mealy bug. If found, wash the soil off the roots and replant into a clean pot; treat with a systemic insecticide.

Take care
Avoid drips from the greenhouse roof during the rest period.

□ Full sun
□ Temp: 5-30°C (41-86°F)
□ Keep dry in winter

Below: Mammillaria spinosissima var. auricoma is one form of this beautiful, widely-grown species. It creates a wealth of richly coloured flowers in summer.

grow an attractive cactus. *N. napina* is quite small, up to 8cm (3.2in) high and 2.5cm (1in) thick, although most specimens are not as large as this. The brownish-green stem is divided into many narrow ribs, arranged in a spiral and with tiny spines. Flowers are large for such a small plant, often 5cm (2in) across, with bright yellow centres. The root is distinctly odd, something like a small turnip, and easily troubled by any excess water. Use a very well-drained potting mixture made up from one part sharp sand or perlite and two parts of a standard peat or loam material. Best to avoid full sun, and water freely on sunny days in spring and summer.

Take care
Use a deep pot for the long root.

☐ Moderate light
☐ Temp: 5-30°C (41-86°F)
☐ Keep dry in winter

Neoporteria napina

Neoporterias are somewhat uncommon cacti, but they are fairly readily available nowadays and well worth growing. They have suffered in the past from the common trouble of name changing, and have been switched from one group to another. However, that need not bother those of us who merely want to

Left: Neoporteria napina comes from Chile and during summer develops large, yellow-centred flowers which, due to their size, often dominate the plant.

Above: Neoporteria nidus develops its reddish flowers amid masses of spines. Well-drained compost is essential to prevent waterlogging and the roots being damaged.

Neoporteria nidus

The cultivation of this little cactus is rather a challenge; it is not one of the easiest, but should not be spurned on that account, as it only needs a good, loving owner! It is a small plant consisting of a solitary, ribbed stem 5-8cm (2-3.2in) in diameter, at first more or less spherical but usually elongating with age. This stem is beautifully clothed with a mass of spines, some long and curved, others slender and almost hair-like. The reddish flowers are fairly easily produced; up to 4cm (1.6in) across.

Cultivation is not really a problem; it merely needs care. Never overwater this cactus, as damp, airless conditions at the root can cause it to disappear. If this happens in spring or summer, cut away all dark tissue, allow to dry for a week, and repot. At any other time of the year leave the repotting until the following spring. Use a particularly well-drained potting mixture made by adding one part of sharp sand or perlite to two parts of a standard mix.

Take care
Give full sun whenever possible.

□ Full sun
□ Temp: 5-30°C (41-86°F)
□ Keep dry in winter

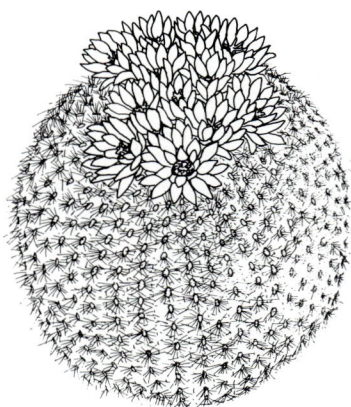

Notocactus haselbergii
BALL CACTUS
SCARLET BALL CACTUS

Notocacti are found growing in the grasslands of South America, and they need full sun. *N. haselbergii* is one of the most beautiful of these cacti. It is a silver ball: the numerous ribs are densely clad in soft white spines, which gleam in the sunshine. It does not form offsets. The flowers are carried on top of the plant in late summer; they are tomato red, an unusual colour in this group of plants. Very young plants do not flower.

N. haselbergii should not be allowed to become too wet, or it may lose its roots. A mixture

Below: Notocactus herteri is neatly rounded and bears some of the most attractive flowers on any notocactus. Keep the compost dry in winter and repot annually.

consisting of one part loam-based potting medium to one part sharp sand or perlite will ensure good drainage. Water freely during summer, but allow it to dry out between waterings. Feed every two weeks with a high-potassium fertilizer during the flowering period. Keep it dry during winter. The only pests likely to be found on this plant are mealy bug and root mealy bug; water with a proprietary insecticide.

Take care
Avoid a wet, soggy potting mix.

□ Full sun
□ Temp: 5-30°C (41-86°F)
□ Water with caution

Notocactus herteri
BALL CACTUS

All the notocacti that have been in cultivation for many years have yellow flowers, but some recently discovered species have beautiful purple flowers, and one of the best of these is *N. herteri*. It is a large globular plant with reddish-brown spines. Although seedlings do not flower, the plant grows quickly and will eventually reach a diameter of at least 15cm (6in). The deep magenta flowers are formed at the top, and open in late summer.

A porous growing mixture consisting of one part loam-based material and one part sharp sand or perlite is suitable. Water freely during the summer, allowing the plant to dry out between waterings. When the buds start to form, feed every two weeks with a high-potassium fertilizer. During winter keep the plant completely dry. It is always advisable to look plants over regularly for the presence of mealy bug: treat with a proprietary insecticide if found.

Take care
Repot annually.

□ Full sun
□ Temp: 5-30°C (41-86°F)
□ Water with care

Oreocereus celsianus

Although wild specimens of this cactus can reach a large size, it is relatively slow-growing, and in the collection it makes a majestic plant, probably eventually reaching a height of around 40cm (16in) and a diameter of 10cm (4in) but taking a number of years to do so from the usual small bought specimens. The cylindrical stem has a number of rounded ribs, and rows of stout, sharp, brownish spines up to 3cm (1.2in) long in larger specimens, and appearing through a mass of silky white hairs. In cultivation this beautiful cactus does not appear to form offsets or branches, so propagation is not practicable; nor is it likely to flower. Enjoy it for itself!

Grow in a standard potting mixture; and although this is not a demanding plant, it is advisable to mix in about one third of sharp sand or perlite, to be on the safe side. Water in spring and summer whenever the potting mixture appears to be drying out.

Take care
In light potting mixtures this plant can become top-heavy.

- □ Full sun
- □ Temp: 5-30°C (41-86°F)
- □ Keep dry in winter

Below: Oreocereus celsianus is an impressive cactus, with contrasting hair and sharp, stout spines. Although slow-growing, it eventually becomes very large.

*Above: A neat, golden ball,
Parodia aureispina freely
produces bright yellow flowers.
Keep the compost dry in winter to
prevent the roots rotting.*

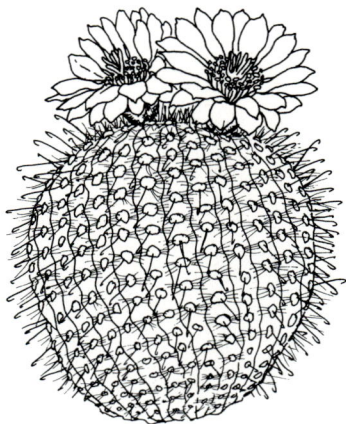

Parodia aureispina
GOLDEN TOM-THUMB CACTUS
TOM-THUMB CACTUS

Parodias are among the most
beautiful of the South American
cacti, but not the easiest to
cultivate. They have a nasty habit
of losing their roots for no
apparent reason. They will regrow
them but the cessation of growth
can leave a scar.

Parodia aureispina is a
beautiful golden ball; the spirally
arranged ribs are densely covered
with short yellow spines, at least
one of which in each group is
hooked. The large buttercup-
yellow flowers are borne on top of
the plant, and open during the
summer. With age the plant
becomes cylindrical and reaches a
height of about 20cm (8in); some
offsets will form.

A porous soil consisting of half
loam-based potting mixture and
half grit will ensure good drainage.
Always allow the soil to dry out
between waterings, and keep the
plant dry during winter. Feed every
two weeks with a high-potassium
fertilizer when the buds form.
Repot annually. Grow in a half-pot
so that the roots are not
surrounded by too much cold, wet
soil.

Take care
Never overwater.

□ Full sun
□ Temp: 5-30°C (41-86°F)
□ Water with great care

Parodia microsperma

Parodia microsperma is globular when young, but with age it becomes elongated. It is a pale green plant with numerous spirally arranged ribs carrying many whitish spines. It will form some offsets, which may be used for propagating the plant. The golden-yellow flowers are about 5cm (2in) across and are carried on the top of the plant during the summer months.

Keep this plant in a sunny position and water it with care during the summer, allowing the soil to dry out before watering again. When buds form feed with a high-potassium fertilizer about every two weeks. Keep dry in

Below: The yellow flowers of Parodia microsperma almost obscure the elegantly spined plant stem. Water with care and keep the compost dry in winter.

winter. Grow in a half-pot in a mixture of one part loam-based mixture to one part grit. Repot annually. The only pests likely to attack parodias are mealy bug and root mealy bug. The odd mealy bug may be picked off with forceps but a bad infestation of either of these pests should be treated with a proprietary insecticide. A systemic one will deal more effectively with root mealy bug.

Take care
Avoid the hooked spines.

□ Full sun
□ Temp: 5-30°C (41-86°F)
□ Water with care

Parodia sanguiniflora

Parodia sanguiniflora, true to its name, has large blood-red flowers. These open in summer, and make a change from the yellow flowers usual in parodias. As a young plant this cactus is globular, but it tends to become cylindrical with age. The numerous spirally arranged ribs carry many brownish spines, some of which are hooked. Some specimens form excessive numbers of offsets to the detriment of flowering. If this happens, restart the plant from an offset. For several years it will flower freely before starting to offset again.

Grow in an open potting mixture, one part loam-based medium to one part grit. Repot annually and inspect the roots for ashy deposits, which indicate root mealy bug; if found, wash off old soil and repot in a clean container. Always water parodias carefully, as they have a tendency to lose their roots if their growing medium becomes excessively wet. Feed with a high-potassium liquid fertilizer every two weeks when in flower. Keep dry during the winter.

Take care
Avoid damp conditions.

□ Full sun
□ Temp: 5-30°C (41-86°F)
□ Water with care

Rebutia muscula

Rebutia muscula is one of the more recently discovered rebutias, and should not be confused with the less attractive R. minuscula. With its clear orange flowers, R. muscula is a beautiful addition to any cactus collection. The flowers open in late spring. The plant body is densely covered with soft white spines. It is a clustering plant and in the sun looks like a silvery cushion. The offsets may be used for propagation.

Like most cacti, R. muscula needs to be grown in strong light. Any loam-based mixture may be used for this plant; to improve the drainage, add one third sharp sand or perlite. During spring and summer water freely, allowing the plant to dry out between waterings. Feed with a high-potassium (tomato) fertilizer every two weeks when buds form.

Mealy bug hide between the clustering heads and suck the sap from the plant. Their white bodies blend with the plant and make discovery difficult.

Take care
Grow in a strong light.

□ Full sun
□ Temp: 5-30°C (41-86°F)
□ Avoid overwatering

for their brightly coloured and distinctive flowers. Many have very small individual heads, but this is one of the larger growing types with heads up to 6cm (2.4in) across and almost as high. By the time the plant has reached this size there will usually be a number of offsets around the base. The deep reddish-purple flowers last for about five days, but because they open in succession, the flowering period may be four weeks.

Use a deep pot to accommodate the long root. Like all sulcorebutias, this plant needs a particularly well-drained potting mixture: up to half its volume of sharp sand or perlite.

Water quite freely in spring and summer, and when it is in full bloom feed every two weeks with a high-potassium fertilizer.

Take care
Waterlogged soil can cause rot.

□ Full sun
□ Temp: 5-30°C (41-86°F)
□ Keep dry in winter

Sulcorebutia totorensis

Sulcorebutias are small, clump-forming, low-growing cacti with large tap-roots; often there is more plant below the soil than above. They are particularly outstanding

Left: Rebutia muscula has many offsets and beautifully coloured flowers amid silky white spines.

Below: Large scarlet flowers make Sulcorebutia totorensis a striking cactus. Good drainage is vital.

Weingartia cumingii

This free-flowering small cactus is sometimes included with *Gymnocalycium,* because of also having hairless flower buds. But, apart from this, the resemblance is not very great. *W. cumingii* is a bright green, spherical plant with a maximum diameter of about 10cm (4in), and divided into a number of spiral, notched ribs. The golden spines are usually less than 1cm (0.4in) long and quite soft and bristly. Deep yellow flowers are freely produced around the top of the stem in spring and summer, about 3cm (1.2in) across.

If you keep this plant indoors, be sure to put it in the coldest room in winter (but with good light) in order to encourage flowering the following year. In a greenhouse there should be no problem. Grow this weingartia in a mixture of good standard material and sharp sand or perlite in the proportion of three to one. Water freely in spring and summer, and give a feed every two weeks with a high-potassium fertilizer.

Take care
Watch for mealy bugs at the base of the flowers.

□ Full sun
□ Temp: 5-30°C (41-86°F)
□ Keep dry in winter

Above: Weingartia cumingii is a particularly free-flowering small cactus, producing masses of blooms in spring and summer. The golden spines are quite soft.

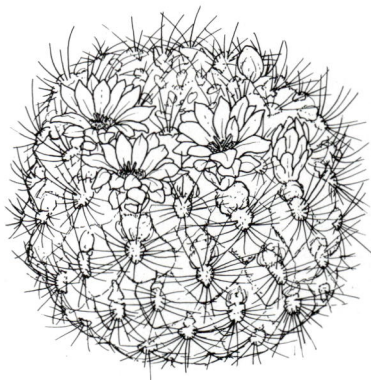

Weingartia lanata

The 'lanata' in the name of this delightful cactus is derived from the clumps of white wool scattered over the stem, which is roughly spherical and reaches a diameter of about 10cm (4in). The spiral ribs are deeply notched so that the appearance is of a mass of large tubercles rather than ribs. It is on the ends of these tubercles that the woolly hair appears, more towards the top of the plant, and also clumps of stiff but not very stout pale brown spines, about 2cm (0.8in) long. For sheer beauty the golden yellow flowers are unsurpassed. Although only about 3cm (1.2in) across, they are produced in profusion around the top of the stem, and in a good year spring or summer flowering is often followed by one in the autumn. The flowers last for several days, but they are scentless.

This is not a demanding cactus, but to be on the safe side add about one third of extra sharp sand or perlite to a good standard mixture. Feed during the flowering period with a high-potassium fertilizer.

Take care
Water freely spring and summer.

□ Full sun
□ Temp: 5-30°C (41-86°F)
□ Keep dry in winter

Difficult to Grow

This section features a range of cacti that will present a real challenge to your skills. All require as much sunlight as possible, for which reason a greenhouse or conservatory is an advantage. Watering is also a very important factor in the plants' care and a dry winter rest is essential, as is a well-draining potting compost.

Those species which bear flowers, such as the sea urchin cactus (*Astrophytum asterias*), need particular attention if they are to be encouraged to bloom. For instance, regular feeding when the plant is in bud is important. A few of the cacti in this section do not bloom readily in cultivation and are simply grown for the beauty of their form; examples include the old man cactus (*Cephalaocereus senilis*) and the cotton ball (*Espostoa lanata*).

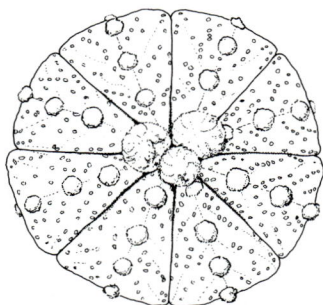

Astrophytum asterias

SAND-DOLLAR
SAND-DOLLAR CACTUS
SEA-URCHIN CACTUS
SILVER-DOLLAR
STAR CACTUS

Astrophytum asterias looks like a grey-green sea urchin; it could never be confused with any other cactus. Eventually it forms a

Above: Cephalocereus senilis is aptly described by its common name, 'old man cactus'. It is covered with a mass of white, beard-like hairs.

flattened hemisphere about 10cm (4in) across. The stem is made up of eight spineless ribs, and the skin is covered with white spots. These vary from plant to plant: some specimens are beautifully covered in white polka dots, whereas others may have very few markings. The flowers open continuously through the summer; they are pale shiny yellow with a red throat, and sweetly scented. Seedlings about 2.5cm (1in) across will flower.

Never overwater and keep the soil completely dry during winter. A very open soil, half loam- or peat-based mixture and half sharp sand or perlite, is suitable. To ensure continuous flowering, keep the plant in the sunniest part of the greenhouse and feed every two weeks with a tomato fertilizer when the buds form.

Take care
Avoid watering on dull days.

□ Full sun
□ Temp: 5-30°C (41-86°F)
□ Do not overwater

Left: An unusual feature of Astrophytum asterias is its spineless, sea-urchin-like stem. It has shiny yellow flowers, making it worth the extra care it needs.

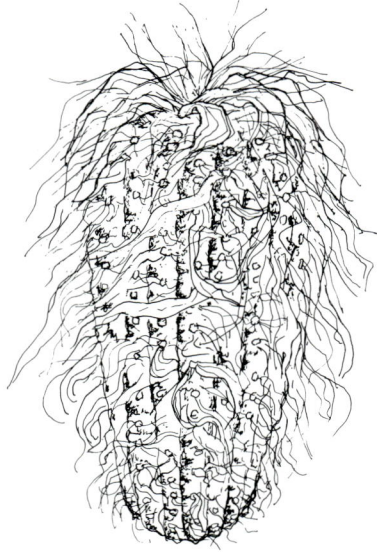

Cephalocereus senilis
OLD MAN CACTUS

In its native Mexico, this cactus forms a column 12m (40ft) high and 45cm (18in) across. These plants are said to be 200 years old, so there is little fear of a seedling outgrowing its accommodation. The white flowers are not produced until the plant is 6m (20ft) high, so this cactus must be grown for the beauty of its form.

The pale green stem with its yellow spines is completely hidden by long, white hairs. These will pick up dust, so to keep the plant gleaming white, shampoo it with a dilute detergent solution and rinse thoroughly; choose a hot sunny day. With advancing age, the lower hairs will inevitably become permanently discoloured. The upper part of the stem may be cut, dried for three days, and potted up. Take cuttings in late spring.

A very open soil — half loam-based mixture and half grit — and a dry winter rest are essential. Keep this cactus in the warmest, sunniest position available.

Take care
Avoid cold, damp conditions.

□ Full sun
□ Temp: 7-30°C (45-86°F)
□ Water very carefully

colour, and the ribs carry glossy black spines that contrast beautifully with the white skin.

Copiapoas need very good drainage; use an open soil, of half loam-based mixture and half sharp sand or perlite. In the winter keep it dry, but during the summer water freely, allowing it to dry out between waterings. Keep this cactus in the sunniest part of the greenhouse; this will keep the plant brightly coloured.

With age, the plant will form offsets along the ribs. These may be used for propagation. *C. cinerea* looks more attractive when grown as a solitary plant.

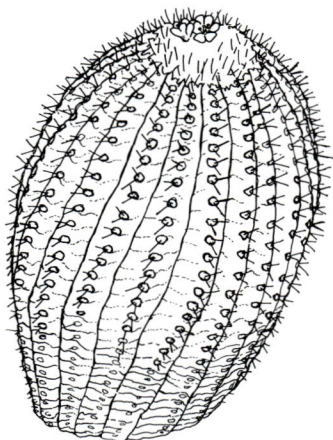

Copiapoa cinerea

Copiapoa cinerea is one of the most beautiful cacti to come out of South America. It is grown for the beauty of its form; it rarely flowers in cultivation, probably because it is difficult to give it sufficient light to stimulate bud formation away from the burning sun of its native desert. Most plants seen in cultivation are the size of a grapefruit. It is chalky-white in

Take care
Avoid damp winter conditions.

□ Full sun
□ Temp: 5-30°C (41-86°F)
□ Water cautiously

Below: Copiapoa cinerea does not readily produce flowers. However, its compact growth and interesting colour make it well worth growing.

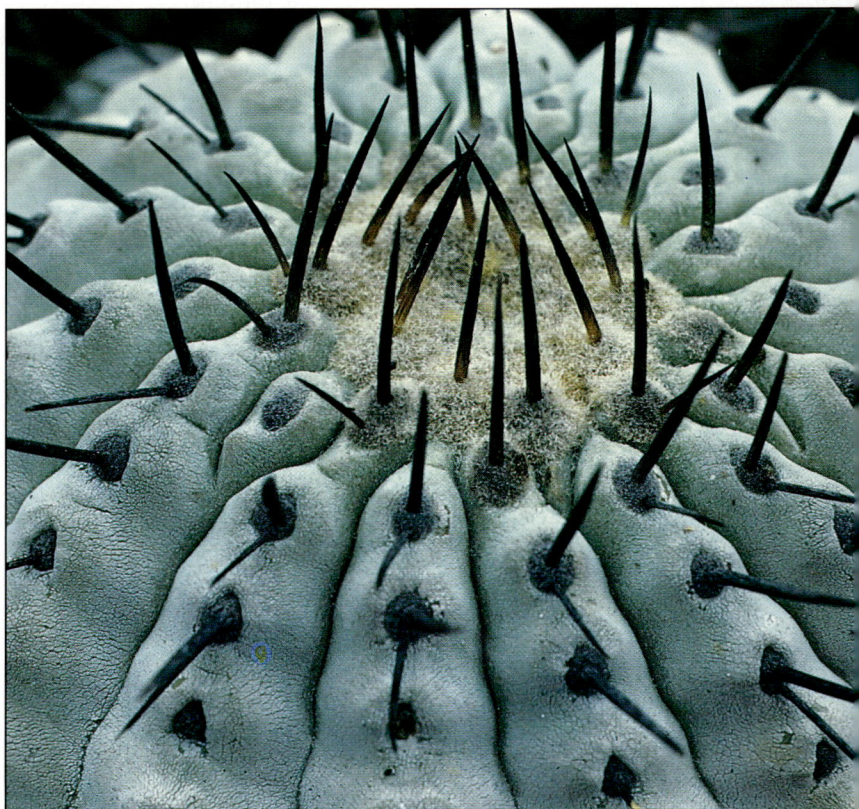

Above: During spring and summer, Echinocereus knippelianus develops deep pink flowers from the side of its dark green stems.

Echinocereus knippelianus

Although this cactus may consist of a single oval or globular stem, about 5cm (2in) thick, for a few years, it will eventually form branches from the base, resulting in a compact clump. The stems have five ribs with a few short, bristly spines along them. Not being fiercely spined, it is quite an easy plant to handle. The deep pink flowers, 4cm (1.6in) or so across, appear from around the sides of the stems in spring and summer, and contrast delightfully with the dark green of the stems. Propagate this cactus by carefully cutting away a branch of at least 2.5cm (1in) across in spring or summer, letting it dry for a few days, and pushing it gently into fresh potting mixture.

Good drainage is essential, so grow this cactus in a mixture of two parts good standard potting material (peat- or loam-based) and one part sharp sand or perlite. When buds form, feed every two weeks with a high-potassium fertilizer.

Take care
Cut out any rotted branch.

□ Full sun
□ Temp: 5-30°C (41-86°F)
□ Keep dry in winter

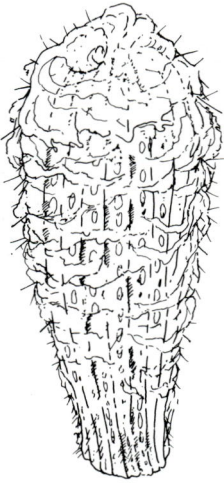

- Full sun
- Temp: 10-30°C (50-86°F)
- Keep dry in winter

Below: This unusual cactus, Espostoa lanata, is covered with a mass of white, woolly hairs. However, under the hairs there are needle sharp spines.

Espostoa lanata

COTTON BALL
NEW OLD MAN CACTUS
PERUVIAN OLD MAN
PERUVIAN SNOWBALL
SNOWBALL CACTUS

Although this cactus can reach tree-like proportions in its native state, 'seedling' plants are perfectly suitable for the collection, where they may reach a height of 30cm (12in) and a thickness of 5cm (2in) but will take many years to reach even this size. Specimens offered for sale are pretty little plants covered with a mass of white woolly hairs. It looks nice enough to stroke, but beware! Under the hair are needle-sharp spines; a trap for the unwary. As the cactus ages, these spines become larger and are visible outside the hair. Do not expect flowers; these are normally produced only on mature plants.

Grow in the usual well-drained potting mixture, made up adding about one third of sharp sand or perlite to a standard material. It is possible to overwinter this cactus in a cool greenhouse at a temperature of 5°C (41°F), but this is risky, and it is better to bring it indoors, unless it is already kept as a houseplant.

Take care
Plants in a window need to be turned.

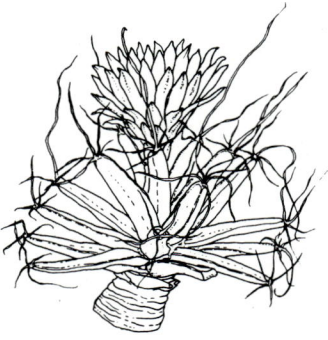

Leuchtenbergia principis
AGAVE CACTUS

A true cactus that bears a remark-
able resemblance to an agave
or aloe, this strange-looking plant is
the sole representative of its group.
Unlike agaves or aloes, the long
tubercles are part of the stem, not
leaves. These tubercles can be up
to 10cm (4in) long and they are
tipped with groups of soft, rather
papery spines. This cactus does not
appear to be very free-flowering,
and to give it the best chance to
produce its beautiful perfumed
yellow flowers, 8cm (3.2in) across,
it needs as much full sunlight as
possible. It is unlikely to flower as a
houseplant. Propagation is said to
be possible from removed
tubercles, dried for a while and
potted up. This is a very easy plant
to raise from seed.

Water this unique cactus freely
in spring and summer, the
tubercles tend to spread when the
plant is moist and to close in with
dryness. Use three parts of a
standard potting mixture added to
one part of sharp sand or perlite.

Take care
Use a deep pot.

□ Full sun
□ Temp: 5-30°C (41-86°F)
□ Keep dry in winter

Below: Two unusual features
which distinguish Leuchtenbergia
principis from all other cacti are
the triangular tubercles and soft
papery, white spines.

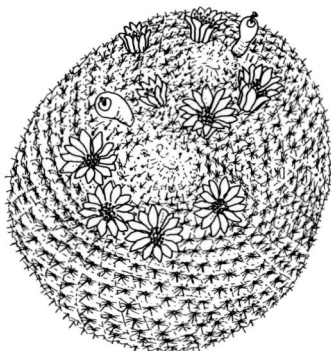

Mammillaria perbella

Mammillaria perbella is a silvery-white cylindrical cactus, about 6cm (2.4in) in diameter, and does not usually branch. The stem is covered in short white spines. The flowering period is early summer, when a ring of flowers appears near the top of the plant. The petals are pale pink with a darker stripe down the middle.

Grow in a mixture of one part loam- or peat-based potting medium and one part sharp sand or perlite. Repot every year and examine the roots for signs of root mealy bug. During spring and summer, water on sunny days, allowing it to dry out between waterings. During the flowering period feed every two weeks with a high-potassium fertilizer. Taper off the watering in autumn and allow the plant to remain dry in winter. Keep this cactus in the sunniest part of your greenhouse; sun stimulates bud formation and spines.

Take care
Do not allow the potting mixture to become hard and compacted.

□ Full sun
□ Temp: 5-30°C (41-86°F)
□ Keep dry in winter

Right: The flowers of Thelocactus bicolor are pale violet with a red throat. Unfortunately, the cactus does not bloom readily and is more often grown for its red and amber spines.

Thelocactus bicolor
GLORY-OF-TEXAS

Although this is not a very large cactus in nature, it does not appear to flower readily in a collection, where the globular stem could reach a diameter of 10cm (4in). Some specimens produce offsets, but others spend solitary lives. Ribs on the stem are divided into notches, giving the effect of low tubercles, carrying the spines that give this cactus its beauty. On each tubercle there is a group of spreading spines up to 2.5cm (1in) long, and four stouter ones somewhat longer. All have the most attractive coloration, red with amber tips (whence the 'bicolor' in its name).

When cultivating thelocactus, use a good standard potting mixture; and add some extra sharp sand or perlite if you have any doubts about its porosity. With such beautiful spines one hardly needs flowers, but if they *do* come they are violet-red in colour. A cold winter rest will encourage them.

Take care
See that no water collects in the crown of this plant.

□ Full sun
□ Temp: 5-30°C (41-86°F)
□ Keep dry in winter

Above: A South American species, Notocactus haselbergii needs full sun and produces masses of tomato-red flowers in late summer. Do not expect young plants to flower, and ensure good drainage.

Index

A
Acanthocalycium violaceum 52
Acclimatizing new plants 8
Agave cactus 91
Aphids, see Woolly aphid
Aporocactus flagelliformis 7, 14
Aporocactus mallisonii 15
Apple cactus 16
Arizona giant 57
Astrophytum asterias 86-87
Astrophytum myriostigma 53
Astrophytum ornatum 54-55

B
Ball cactus 19, 36, 38, 76-77
Barrel cactus 19, 24-25, 60
Beaver-tail cactus 39
Bishop's cap 54-55
Bishop's cap cactus 53
Bishop's-hood 53
Bishop's mitre 53
Borzicactus aureiflora 56
Brain cactus 23
Bunny-ears 40
Buying cacti, advice on 7

C
Carnegiea gigantea 57
Cephalocereus senilis 86-87
Cereus peruvianus 16
Chamaecereus silvestrii 7, 16-17
Chin cactus 28-30, 64-68
Cholla cactus 39-43
Christmas cactus 7, 14, 49
Cleistocactus strausii 7, 18
Cob cactus 32, 69-70
Compost, advice on 10
Copiapoa cincerea 88
Corky scab 13
Coryphantha vivipara 58
Cotton ball 86, 90
Crown cactus 46

D
Dactylopius coccus 12
Devil's-tongue 62
Display, advice on 11-12

E
Easter-lily cactus 24-25
Echinocactus grusonii 7, 19
Echinocereus knippelianus 89
Echinocereus pentalophus 20-21
Echinocereus perbellus 59
Echinocereus salm-dyckianus 20-21
Echinocereus websterianus 22
Echinofossulocactus lamellosus 23
Echinopsis aurea 24
Echinopsis eyriesii 25
Echinopsis multiplex 24-25
Echinopsis Paramount hybrid
  'Orange Glory' 26
Epiphyllum 'Ackermannii' 26-27
Epiphyllum 'Cooperi' 28
Espostoa lanata 86, 90

F
Feeding, advice on 9
Ferocactus acanthodes 60
Ferocactus horridus 61
Ferocactus latispinus 62
Fire-crown cactus 48
Fish-hooks cactus 33, 60
Frailea asteroides 63
Frailea castanea 63

G
Giant cactus 57
Giant saguaro 57
Glory-of-Texas 93
Golden ball 19
Golden ball cactus 19, 36
Golden barrel cactus 7, 19
Golden column 51
Golden-lace cactus 34
Golden-star cactus 34
Golden Tom-Thumb cactus 79
Gold lace cactus 34
Goldplush 40
Gymnocalycium andreae 64
Gymnocalycium baldianum 65
Gymnocalycium bruchii 28-29
Gymnocalycium denudatum 66
Gymnocalycium horridispinum 67
Gymnocalycium mihanovichii
  'Hibotan' 30
Gymnocalycium quehlianum 68

H
Hamatocactus setispinus 31
Heliaporus smithii 15

I
Infestation 13

L
Lace cactus 34
Lady finger cactus 34
Leuchtenbergia principis 91
Lobivia aurea 24
Lobivia backebergii 69
Lobivia densispina 70
Lobivia hertrichiana 32
Lobivia silvestrii 16

M
Mammillaria bocasana 33
Mammillaria bombycina 52, 71
Mammillaria elongata 34
Mammillaria perbella 52, 92
Mammillaria spinosissima 72-73
Mammillaria spinosissima var.
  auricoma 72-73
Mammillaria zeilmanniana 35
Matucana aureiflora 56
Mealy bug 13
Monkshood 53

N
Neoporteria napina 74
Neoporteria nidus 75

New old man cactus 90
Notocactus haselbergii 76-77, 94
Notocactus herteri 76-77
Notocactus leninghausii 36-37
Notocactus ottonis 38

O
Old man cactus 86-87
Opuntia basilaris 39
Opuntia microdasys 40
Opuntia robusta 41
Opuntia salmiana 42
Opuntia scheerii 43
Orchid cactus 7, 26-28
Oreocereus celsianus 78
Ornamental monkshood 54-55

P
Parodia aureispina 79
Parodia microsperma 80-81
Parodia sanguiniflora 81
Peanut cactus 7, 16-17
Pereskia aculeata 44-45
Peruvian apple 16
Peruvian apple cactus 16
Peruvian old man 90
Peruvian snowball 90
Pests 13
Physiological disorders 13
Pink Easter lily 24-25
Plain cactus 30
Positioning, advice on 10
Powder-puff cactus 33
Prickly pear 39-43

R
Rabbit-ears 40
Rat's tail cactus 7, 14
Rebutia albiflora 46
Rebutia calliantha var. *krainziana* 47
Rebutia minuscula 82
Rebutia muscula 82
Rebutia senilis 48
Red spider mite 13

Repotting, advice on 10
Rhipsalis baccifera 6
Root knot eelworm 13
Root mealy bug 13
Rose-pincushion 35
Rose tuna 39
Ruby ball 30

S
Saguaro 57
Sand-dollar 86-87
Sand-dollar cactus 86-87
Scale insect 12-13
Schlumbergera 'Buckleyi' 7, 14, 49
Sea-urchin cactus 24-26, 86-87
Silver-dollar 86-87
Silver torch 7, 18
Snowball cactus 33, 90
Spider cactus 66
Star cactus 54-55, 86-87
Stenocactus 23
Sulcorebutia totorensis 83

T
Temperature, advice on 10
Thelocactus bicolor 93
Tom-Thumb cactus 79
Torch cactus 16, 51
Trichocereus chilensis 50
Trichocereus spachianus 51

UV
Violet sea-urchin 52
Viruses 13

W
Watering, advice on 9-10
Weingartia cumingii 84
Weingartia lanata 85
White torch cactus 51
Woolly aphid 12-13

XYZ
Yellow bunny ears 40

Picture Credits

The publishers wish to thank the following photographers and agencies for supplying photographs for this book. Photographs have been credited on the page: (B) Bottom, (T) Top.

A-Z Botanical Collection: 36-37, 60, 78(B), 87
Heather Angel: 7, 12(B)
Eric Crichton: Front cover
Terry Hewitt: 15, 18(T), 18-19(B), 22, 30(T), 30-31(B), 32-33(T), 32-33(B), 41, 44-45, 56, 59, 63, 68(B),
68-69(T), 70, 71, 74
Keith Laban: 16-17, 26-27
Frans Noltee: 1, 3, 14, 20-21(B), 38(T), 43, 46-47(B), 47(T), 52,78-79(T), 83, 86, 88, 92-93, 94
Gordon Rowley: Back cover, 5, 20(T), 23, 24, 28-29, 38-39(B), 48, 50-51, 53, 54-55, 57, 58, 61, 62, 64-65(T), 64-65(B), 66, 67, 76-77, 80-81, 84-85, 89, 91
Harry Smith Horticultural Photographic Collection: 6, 8, 9, 11, 12(T), 25, 34, 35, 40, 42, 49, 72-73, 75, 82, 90